The Way Out Book

by John-Roger

Cover Art by Josie Lander
Illustrations by Su-Zan

I.S.B.N. 0-914829-23-8

Copyright ©1980, 1984, 1986 by
John-Roger

Published by Baraka Press, Inc.
P.O. Box 3935
Los Angeles, CA 90051

Printed in the United States of America

First Printing
10,000 copies

Second Printing
8,500 copies

Special thanks go to Su-Zan,
Jeri Duckworth and Connie Feldman
for their loving support and invaluable
production assistance and to Theresa
Hocking for compiling the index.

BOOKS BY THE AUTHOR

Baraka
Blessings of Light
Buddha Consciousness
The Christ Within
The Consciousness of Soul
A Consciousness of Wealth
Disciples of Christ
Drugs
Dynamics of the Lower Self
Inner Worlds of Meditation
The Journey of a Soul
Manual on Using the Light
The Master Chohans of the Color Rays
Passage Into Spirit
The Path to Mastership
Possessions, Projections, and Entities
The Power Within You
The Signs of the Times
The Spiritual Family

Available through
BARAKA BOOKS
P.O. Box 3935
Los Angeles, CA 90051

This book
is dedicated to
Rev. Pauline McGarry

TABLE OF CONTENTS

INTRODUCTION

The Way Out Book is a practical guide to becoming more aware of your spirituality. If the idea of "being spiritual" is attractive to you and if you have felt that yearning to know more about your self and your God — but have been "turned off" by organized religions, strange cults and weird rituals — this book may be for you.

The ideas and techniques presented in this book are ways that I have found work for me. In sharing them with people over the last couple of decades, many others have discovered these ideas work for them. People are living their lives according to spiritual law, not because I tell them to or because anyone else tells them to, but because it's a way that brings health, wealth, happiness, joy, and fulfillment to them in much greater measure.

The words written in this book won't solve your problems for you. They won't solve anything at all. They may give you some guidelines and directions that will assist **you** in solving your own problems. If anything at all is required, it's just that you check these things out for yourself. Be your own scientific investigator, and see what results you discover.

The subjects included in The Way Out Book are diverse, and touch upon many aspects of human conscious-

1

ness, many problems, and many situations that we all deal with in our lives. They present ideas for dealing successfully with these situations, the ultimate idea being that knowledge of yourself and of the God within you will allow you to deal successfully with anything. There are many paths to that awareness and knowledge. If one works for you and another doesn't, choose the one that does, and bypass the one that doesn't. It's not necessary to agree with, much less believe in, everything in this book to gain value from one aspect of it. My suggestion is that you be open in your approach to this material and accept the possibility that it may be accurate. Then check it out, and if it is true for you, make it part of your living experience. That is a good way to validate this information and make it work for you.

Before we begin, let me give you a brief explanation of some of the premises that are the foundation for the content of this book. Again, you don't have to believe these ideas, but know that they are the basis for my approach. You might want to play the "What if" game as you read this book. "What if" the ideas presented are true? "What if" the concepts presented here are accurate? Try them on; see if they fit.

Men and women—all men and women—are spiritual beings. We are all of God. There is nothing and no one that is not of God. The spark of God individualized within human beings is the Soul. The Soul is the basic element of our existence. The Soul is forever connected to God. That connection is perfect and intimate; it is the source from which we draw our life. The nature, the essence, of the Soul is JOY. It is joyful because it is wholly of God, is aware of that, and has total knowledge of that.

The human consciousness is a different matter. There are many elements in addition to the Soul that make up the human consciousness. These elements can sometimes cloud the clarity of spiritual vision and interfere with our ability to perceive God directly. These elements are the body, the

2

imagination, the mind, the emotions, the subconscious, and the unconscious.

The elements of human consciousness are actually microcosms of greater universes. Thus, there are many planes or realms of existence beyond the physical universe we see with our eyes. Some realms are of a positive nature and some are of a negative nature. Much like the positive and negative polarities on a battery, it is the combination of positive and negative that creates movement, action, the dynamics of life as we know it. The human consciousness has different tools for different levels.

If you want to see how things are separated into their own levels, think about using your emotions to move a tree out of your path. It can't be done. The tree is physical; it is not existing on the emotional level. Therefore your emotions have no power over that tree. If you wish to move it out of your path, you must come into a physical expression and move it physically.

We have a physical body, which is a tool for the physical level. With the body, we can manipulate this level. We can move through space. We can move objects. The body is our vehicle for our life here on the physical realm. We have an imagination, which is our tool for the astral level of consciousness. In our imaginations we can "see" different scenes. We can mock up or create all sorts of things. We can create pleasant scenes; we can create nightmares. These creations have life and power, as we give it to them, on the astral realm. The imagination is our vehicle on that level.

The emotions are the tool for the causal level of consciousness. We exist and move on that level through our emotions. We can influence other people's emotions with our emotions. They are a very powerful tool.

3

On the mental level of consciousness, the mind is your tool. You can create thoughts. You can cognize theories. You can use logic, deduction, induction...there are many processes of the mind. The mind is your vehicle for the mental realm. Have you ever tried to explain away an emotion and found that it just continues to exist no matter how much you **think** it should go away? These levels often overlap and intertwine, but they definitely have distinct and separate characteristics.

The unconscious levels of your being are your vehicle to the etheric realm of consciousness. This is a difficult area to discuss, pin down, or perceive, because it is unconscious. There are aspects that become known to you, however, through your experience of this level. The area of the subconscious and unconscious has been probed for years by the psychiatrists and psychologists, and it is still an elusive area. One key to the awareness of this level is to know that it is not functioning as the body, imagination, emotions, or mind. So attempting to identify the processes of the unconscious from these other levels is usually futile. Knowledge of the unconscious comes with the **experience** of the unconscious.

The Soul is your vehicle for the pure, positive realms of Spirit. The Soul knows Spirit and God directly. Again, it is not a process of body, imagination, emotions, mind, or unconscious, although it may use these aspects of human consciousness as a tool. It is a direct experience of the reality of beingness. It is an experience of the infinite and cannot be perceived by that which is finite.

I work with the Light; I teach my students to work with the Light. We use the Light to direct ourselves into God. The Light is the energy of Spirit that pervades all levels of consciousness. It is an energy that is of God. It is pure, uncorrupted, and available for our use. We use the Light to become more aware of ourselves and all our levels of being, to direct ourselves through all levels, always keeping in mind that our goal is Soul awareness. As we direct our lives into the highest expression we know, in clarity and in purity, then we are more consciously aware of the Light. We more directly experience the Soul and the God that is the source of all Light. That experience of Soul then floods down through all the levels of unconscious, mind, emotions, imagination, and body, and we discover that all those levels may be used to enhance our experience of Soul. Nothing is separate; all is one. Each level serves its purpose and may exist in harmony and balance with all others, creating a joyful, balanced, integrated and loving human being.

Within each level there are lessons to be learned. Each lesson points toward greater knowledge of that level, thus greater understanding, thus greater freedom. If the lessons are not learned, there are other opportunities for learning. These cycles of opportunities relate to the concepts of karma and reincarnation.

Let's say that you have accumulated quite a lot of wealth during your life. You have two choices. You can use that wealth and abundance to enhance your life and the lives of those around you. Or you can use that wealth to create patterns of fear, distrust and anxiety. You can use the wealth wisely, keeping your life in balance with those around you. Or you can hoard the wealth, wield it as power over those around you, use it to blackmail, and control and subjugate. One use is positive; the other negative.

Using your wealth negatively indicates that you have not discovered the true nature of your wealth; you have not learned the lesson of handling abundance with loving. And that lesson will be there for you to learn another time. Perhaps, at a later time, you will be in the reverse position. You might be poor and destitute and at the mercy of one who is wealthy and uses that wealth to put you down. In this way, the lesson is learned from the opposite side of the experience, and your former abuse of wealth may be balanced. In essence, this is the law of karma that functions here on the physical realm.

If you use your wealth in a balanced way, if you use it as an extension of your loving, if you use it to uplift and to enhance your life and others' lives, you have demonstrated that you know the nature of abundance; the lesson is learned, the karma is balanced, and you are clear in your consciousness.

The law of karma, taken beyond the context of a single life, is the foundation for reincarnation. Often the imbalances that you have created in your life through abuse and misuse of many aspects of your consciousness cannot be balanced in one lifetime. So the consciousness returns to this level to fulfill the debts incurred and balance the action. The law of karma is a just and perfect system and ensures that those who evolve into the Soul consciousness have a deep and true knowledge of all levels of consciousness. This physical level is the "lab." To graduate, you must demonstrate your knowledge and your understanding of all the processes involved here. "Book learning" will not get you free. Your experience is your teacher that leads you to freedom.

I do not teach retreat from life. I do not teach renunciation of life. I encourage full participation in life, because it is through your participation in your life that you discover yourself and learn the lessons that are necessary to your evolvement.

This book offers you keys to your own life so that your experience may become more valuable to you. It offers you some "rules to the game." This life came without a set of instructions on how to live it. You may have figured out that it's a game, but it may seem like someone hid the rulebook. When the rules are made more clear, it's a whole lot easier to play and to win this game we call "life."

If you would find the
Kingdom of Heaven,
look within.
If you would find the
peace of God,
look within.
These things are not
separate from you.

The Kingdom
Lies Within

Chapter One

How do you receive enlightenment? How does it happen? Many ways. Do you get it through yourself? Yes. Do you get it by yourself? Always. What if you don't know where to get it? Those who are enlightened can point the way. Their great value is that they can be wayshowers — not teachers, wayshowers.

It can become discouraging and disturbing when people who are moving toward enlightenment, but who are not yet there, get the "holy man's disease": "My enlightenment is better than yours." And, really, how can that be judged? Is from fifty to ninety doing well? From thirty to forty just making it? I don't think it can be graded that way. If it could, some people might feel very secure to think that by using the "correct" vocabulary they could ensure having God in their corner. "Turn to page thirty-two... that's God." But it doesn't happen that way at all.

When you come to the realization, inwardly, that you need to find God, how do you go about that? You find God through yourself. You find God by yourself. People who are following Jesus may say, "Jesus will save you." But who has to make the first step? **You** have to make that first step toward your own salvation. **You** have to make the commitment to let Jesus save you. In essence, that is saving yourself. You always have to assume responsibility for yourself.

9

People say that their gurus will save them. But no guru, no teacher, will work with you toward enlightenment unless you let him know that you are interested. So you go to a teacher and tell him that you are interested; you ask him to save you. He may say, "Okay," but he will also say, "Then do these things I ask of you." Jesus said, "Do these things." All teachers say, "Do these things." And they are all pointing out the unity underlying all things. Every one of them will tell you that there are causes and effects and that **you** are the cause and **you** are the effect.

Those who are traveling the Surat Shabd know that in MSIA we deal with the Sound Current of God. That is our path. The Bible tells us that the Word (which is the Sound) was made flesh. Others call it the Logos. It doesn't matter what the words are because it is the essence of God with which we are working.

We also work with the Light of God in a process of living love. If you follow any path and do not find the love of God on that path, then leave it and seek out one that carries the love. There must be love of God and love for God. There must be love for the Light consciousness that comes through all people, for that is God. If you say you love one person but not another, you cannot say that you love God. You can have love for all, but prefer certain people close to you, and still love God. It is your responsibility to live in preferences and discernment.

When you discern your preference levels, you are not discriminating against the rest. That is not a play on words, either. That is an actuality. The life of preference is the life of discernment. You cannot establish preferences unless you have the ability to discern. And you cannot discern clearly unless you have some knowledge of the subject at hand. The physical body discerns physical bodies, and the basic selves discern other basic selves. Emotions discern emotions, and the mind discerns the mind. The Soul discerns the Soul and everything below it.

How do you ever reach the level above you if the mechanism and the tools you have present cannot see above and so cannot get you there? Light bearers and wayshowers come to show you the vision of enlightenment, the vision of Soul transcendence. You may not be able to tell if they are phonies or frauds, but you can work their information, anyway, and see if it awakens you.

The challenge is present. Regardless of who tells you, regardless of whether or not you believe it, if you can work the information and move your own awareness higher, you are moving toward enlightenment. You have to go to those levels of Spirit, however, to receive an awakening of Spirit. It is difficult to go to a mathematics book to discern Spirit. (Actually, you could, if you understood that it is infinity that you are dealing with in all equations. If you stop short of that concept, you're caught in numbers and figures, and that is not of Spirit.)

To discern Spirit, you must attune yourself to Spirit and to those who know Spirit. It is an eternal struggle, because on this physical level you have the body, emotions, mind, unconscious, and subconscious all thrusting to bind the Soul to this level. The Soul, on this physical level, is the weakest element, which explains why we sometimes fall apart. Yet, that which is weakest on this level endures the longest. When you get up into the Soul realm, the Soul becomes the strongest element. The rules change; the Soul wins. It will always win because it is the Soul that endures past all things. The Soul in the Soul realm is positive energy in a positive realm, and its strength cannot be matched. But here on earth, the Soul is positive energy in a negative realm, and the negative elements appear to have greater strength.

As long as you believe in and give power to the illusions of this world, you will get caught up in them. This isn't bad; it may be that the cause and effect with which you are dealing is going to hold you into the earth plane for

11

a few more lessons, for a few more experiences. Love them. The key to breaking free is to love yourself and to love each experience that comes to you whether it appears to be negative or positive. Love it all equally.

If someone comes up to you and says, "I don't think you're so smart," love that person. He can't do much in the face of pure love. You may not love what he's doing or saying; you may not love his expression. But somewhere inside of you, you can still love that person. You may love him far away from you. That's fine. You have a right to select whom you have close to you. You can love people and not have them all in your front room. You can love them in their front rooms.

Being spiritual doesn't mean that you have to be "namby-pamby" or weak. The spiritual path is not necessarily an easy one. It can be difficult. For instance, it's often "open game" for every religionist, agnostic, atheist, or anyone else who may not see things as you do. It takes great strength to walk the spiritual path in the truth and honesty of your own consciousness.

With greater spiritual awareness comes greater responsibility to Spirit, and this means to the Spirit everywhere. It is your responsibility to be true to the spiritual essence that you have discovered within. It is stated in all scripture—the Bible as well as the scriptures of the Eastern religions—to let your light shine among men and let your good works speak for you.

You have a responsibility to be loving. And often you can do that silently more effectively than you can do it verbally. It's important to be loving in whatever situation you find yourself. Even husbands and wives have no right to hurt each other. They don't get married for that purpose. They are married to become a fortress, possibly to rear children and to create a retreat from the world where they can renew their strength. The family environment can be used to gain the strength necessary to go back out into the world and learn to work with energy to break the conditioning of the world. If you come home after a "hellish" day at work and get hell from your wife or husband, that is really hell. Then you don't want to come home at all. It is your responsibility to be loving— not to let yourself be taken advantage of—but to be loving in all your relationships.

Love is the key to awakening to the Spirit within. Sometimes you don't even know when you are asleep, in the spiritual sense. It takes discernment to recognize the level of your enlightenment and then seek out those who can show you the next level. That part that is awake is the Soul. It never sleeps. It is in a constant state of pure awareness. The mind sleeps, the emotions sleep, the body sleeps. As you realize this, you wonder if you're really as great as you sometimes think you are. You're *not* great in the sense of your ego, but in the Soul you are far greater than you think you are. Thoughts cannot conceive the greatness of the Soul. You can't find the majesty of the Soul in science books or math books. You may not even be able to consciously look and find a key that awakens something inside of you a little more than before. So all you can do is let go and say, "It's beyond my mental ability."

Be with those people who are lifting to Spirit. Let them share with you, but realize that each person's way is special for that person. Don't compare levels of what you call spirituality. Sit and listen and support each person with your love and your joy for them. Then move back to your own truth, to your own work, to your own beingness. Within you is the kingdom of God. You have the key. As you awaken more fully to the consciousness of God, you find that there is no love or lover. There is only the Beloved.

Awakening Soul

I f you find that you love God, you are separate from God. If you find God loving you, you are separate. It is when you find you **are** the Beloved that you become the path. You become the Light, the Truth and the Way. There is no separation; there is only the Beloved.

When a Soul is stirred to awaken, to move on into its greater awareness, the paradoxes of life are placed before it to see if, in the expression of this part of God's kingdom, it can indeed express Godliness. And because this physical level is a composite of all levels (physical, imaginative, emotional, mental, and unconscious), we can clear things faster from this level than from any other level below the Soul. So the Soul brings together the elements necessary to create a physical embodiment. The Soul can do this; the Soul, being divine, can do anything it wishes to do. It embodies onto this physical realm because it knows it can reveal itself faster from here than from any other level.

The Soul is a powerful creator. It brings forward those things for which the consciousness asks, whether in this lifetime or in another lifetime. Yet that which you have asked for often cannot be given to you here on this physical level. So you must wait until you reach the other levels to get it. If you have asked for things of a physical nature and leave this body before getting them, you may go to the astral realm, the realm closest to the physical, and get that which you asked for. And when you get it there, it can become greatly disturbing to your astral body. So you seek the purification from that. This purification is traditionally called "hell" or "purgatory", which isn't a negative process. It's the purification. It's getting rid of the last entanglements of the physical level.

God, in His perfect consciousness, has placed out certain patterns that each individualized consciousness, each Soul, must fulfill. And all humans will fulfill the patterns in their own timing. There are more rapid ways and less rapid ways. If, indeed, you can be taught, the Soul will awaken itself on the physical level and dissolve all karmic bondage. Then you will be aware of Soul on this level and on all other levels. At that moment, you become what we call the "living free." There will not be one thing you can do that will not be perfect in the sight of God — not one thing. And you won't do anything that would not be in balance with who you are and where you are. Other people may look at you or your actions and condemn you, but what does that matter. They're condemning everybody — not just you. When I hear somebody saying something negative about me, I just look at them, knowing that if they are talking about me, they're talking about everyone. Why should I have concern because they've singled out me? Their gossip will come back to them to be worked out at another time because that is the law.

It's nice to recognize that the Soul holds itself responsible for all its actions and creations. The consciousness may try to "get away with something" or may try to fool itself and lull itself into patterns of unawareness, but the Soul says, "These things I am. These are things for which I am responsible. These things I will fulfill right down to the last farthing." The Soul fulfills all things within itself.

The Soul, the essence of God within, is responsible. Ultimately, it is the author of all your actions. So pass the authorship to where it belongs. Jesus said, "Of myself I can do nothing. The Father within does all things." The Father is the God within or the Soul or whatever term you care to use. Often we call it the Light. Jesus said that he was the Light and the Truth and the Way. Buddha said

15

that he was the Light of Asia. The Light that springs eternally is the Light of which we are speaking. It is the pure energy of Spirit.

When the Soul leaves the physical realm and starts upward, it becomes very easy to drop the imagination, very easy to drop the emotions and very easy to drop the mind. But when you get to the etheric level (the unconscious), you may look into the unconscious and see it reflect back to you the glories of the earth. Then you may enter into an identification with that glory and reincarnate. One way to break through the realm of the unconscious into Soul is to be working with one who has the keys, the knowledge and the ability to show you the illusion of the unconscious and the way through it into Soul. Often the unconscious is so strong in its pulling back to the physical, in the remembrance of the emotions and the desires, that the consciousness will not heed the wayshower, and it steps back into reembodiment.

When you get up very high from the earth, it looks like a paradise, a garden of Eden. I think one of the astronauts said this when he was quite high above the earth. When you get up high in your consciousness and look back, you may say, "Wow, that's paradise!" and impel yourself back again. There are a lot of reasons why the Soul keeps coming back. In a way, it is a paradise here, but it is not as yet in the higher realms of Light and love. You can live here in the physical body and reside in heaven by being aware of both levels simultaneously. How do you do that? You get enough experience of this level; you develop a knowing of what this level is. Then you stop doing this, and you automatically start doing that.

To know consciously of the other side, you must shut your mouth to this side. You must not be the teacher. You must be the student. When you explain something to someone, don't feel that they **have** to understand it, that they **have** to get it. That's cramming it down their throats, and no one is going to swallow that. You present a point of view to them and let them look at it. If they don't move on it, perhaps it wasn't for them. Perhaps they've already moved on it in another dimension. Perhaps they are yet to experience that moving. Noninterference is so very important. It is so important to allow each consciousness, each Soul, the freedom to evolve into its own awareness in its own timing.

Before Mahatma Gandhi was released from the physical body, he knew very well that his assassination was coming. A detective said, "Let me protect you; let me go with you." Mahatma Gandhi asked what else he would bring with him. He said, "My gun." Gandhi said, "Don't come with your gun; leave your gun." The detective said, "I can't do that. I couldn't protect you without my gun." Gandhi said, "Then it isn't you who protects me; it's your gun." Force does not work. But as we just stand beside another person and support them with our love and Light, that helps. Gandhi was not going to let anybody interfere with the order of things, lest someone be shot in his name. Within his consciousness he would much rather be murdered than be the murderer. Gandhi was a great Soul and knew his Soul in consciousness.

The same awareness of Soul is ours for the taking, but we must do it. We must manifest the same teachings that have been taught all along. Love is. It is noninterfering. It is supporting. It's that which says, "Look, I may not understand everything going on, but that doesn't mean you can't do it, just because I don't understand it." Love is, "I don't know the words and the vocabulary seems strange to me, but that doesn't mean it's not valid and can't be worked." The first time I heard the dialect of an African country, I said, "I certainly don't know what is being said, but the people who are communicating do." And sometimes you'll hear people talking about physics or computer sciences and say, "I can't understand a word they say, but they know." Those who are doing it understand. Maybe you don't need to understand computer programming. Maybe you need to understand yourself. And when you do this, you find out what it's like to walk with the Beloved. God bestows grace upon every Soul because God bestows grace upon Itself. And through that grace, God is saying, "Everything is all right."

Discovering Peace

As you begin your search for enlightenment, for knowledge of God and the experience of Spirit, you may look in many places. And you will probably experience much disappointment as you search "out there" for your answers. Two thousand years ago, Jesus the Christ said, "The kingdom of Heaven lies within." He spoke the truth and gave us one of the greatest keys to enlightenment. If you would find the kingdom of Heaven, look within. If you would find the peace of God, look within. These things are not separate from you.

When you move to the power source of your beingness in the inner kingdom, you find happiness and joy. It is a dynamic joy, an active expression of happiness. And within that happiness is peace. It may not be jovial or raucous happiness, but it is one where the warmth of your own consciousness is united with the knowingness of your Soul. And when those two aspects are one, happiness is the natural result.

When you seek out in the world for happiness or peace, you are moving into patterns of self-denial because you are, in actuality, saying that peace does not reside naturally within yourself. So you come from a consciousness of lack, and lack is the result. When you go into the outer world seeking peace, you are looking for sensation. Sensation, for a short time, can assuage the yearning for peace. It can distract you momentarily, but it's not long before the sensations of the world stupify your physical senses, and you find yourself automatically retreating back toward yourself. You find yourself yearning for peace.

There are many people who live the "good life," have successful businesses, great wealth, and all the security this world has to offer...and what they would like more than all of that is peace of mind. They say, "I'd give anything if my mind would leave me alone so I could gather my strength and feel good inside myself." That peace is your natural state, but if you look out into the world for sensation, you can obscure that peaceful quality within.

When people fight, they are actually attempting to bring harmony and balance into their situation. They are attempting to find peace. That's why they fight. Tradition has told you that if you yell louder than the other guy, you'll win, and then you'll have peace and contentment. Have you found out it doesn't work that way? You make your point. He shuts up — and then waits for his chance to get back at you. And he'll do it when you're most vulnerable; he'll attack your weakest area and destroy that which you thought was your peace.

When you seek for power in this world, there will always be people coming from behind you to usurp that power. They will take the power from you. If you have established peace within your own consciousness, **no one** can take that from you. They won't even be able to find it, and they certainly won't be able to dislodge it.

When you awaken each morning, it might be nice if you ask for the peace of God to be with you and all you touch that day. If you are one with God's consciousness, no man can come against you. If you ask for this attunement each day (and it doesn't matter what words you use), it will change the quality of your life. You may find yourself talking less. To find the peace within, it's often necessary to become quiet verbally so that you can hear the voice of love from within that tempers all associations in the other world.

The sanctuary of the heart is the location of peace. You move into the spiritual heart to discover peace. God speaks to you through your heart. God brings peace to your life. You can know happiness, and you can know love. There is nothing else worth knowing. Love is the only channel for clear communication. And peace is the parent of love.

Sensation is the other end of the spectrum. It is the opposite of peace. The reason so many people find themselves in an endless search for sensation is because they must confront themselves if they move inward to find the peace. That's what makes the quality of peace and love so difficult to find. You decide you want to find peace, you start tuning within, and you find all your troubles, your hurts, your pain, and your disturbances. So you think, "I'm not going to do that; that hurts!" And you go back out into the world. You bum around, run around, and make excuses to go here and there. Yet, when you finally stop, your irritation is still with you.

We often tell people to sit still and do something, rather that sit still and do nothing. Sitting still and doing **something** means that you are looking within for balance. When the emotions surge on you and you have fear, you look at that fear. You trace it back within you to find the source. If you remember a hurt from the past, you follow that hurt and find out what happened that caused it. Then it can be cleared from that level. When the Light of God becomes manifest in your consciousness, you will also experience illusion. They go side by side. You will experience both, and there can be great confusion in that.

If people ask you what it is like in China this time of year, can you tell them? Maybe you haven't been to China but have seen pictures taken this time of year, so tell them you've seen pictures. Don't lead them to believe that you **know** from your own experience. Or if you've talked to someone who has been there, you might say that you heard from someone that it's nice this time of year...but again, don't try to make them think it has been your experience. If you **have** been in China, you will be able to tell them much

21

more completely what it is like. You will be able to tell of special experiences which would be unknown to you if you had only seen a picture or heard a friend's experience. Someone else's experience is always a reflection. Your own experience is your reality.

The physical world is always a reflection. Your inner world is the reality. The physical world is represented by the sensation. The inner world is represented by peace and happiness. And love. As you tune to that inner world, you find that you begin to experience peace. The emotions subside, the mind becomes more quiet. And you may find, from deep within your beingness, you open yourself to receive that which is of God. You may feel the Spirit touch to you; you may hear a voice whisper, "Be still and know that I am God." And you will know that you are awakening to your Self more and more.

 # Bringing All Things Present

Y ou may, at times, find yourself sitting, thinking of nothing in particular, in a stream of consciousness, one thought flowing into another freely, spontaneously. You may not be feeling much of anything at all, and you certainly do not want to be identified with the body. You may be reaching into a state of natural high, of euphoria, where you start to discover the joy of Spirit that comes the closest to a "state of being."

Joy, dynamically moving through your consciousness, changing, altering, updating, making all things new, is indicative of the presence of Spirit. The Spirit is always NOW, always present. When you are most aware of it, you are also wholly present, at one with the Spirit within. Those are the moments when Spirit is most mobile within you, and you are able to most clearly identify yourself as an extension of the divine.

If your consciousness is locked into yesterday, the Spirit is less mobile within you. It is locked in, not free to be in the flow of this moment NOW. To hold it to yesterday, you have to press against it, and often you also have to press against other people to remind them, "Yesterday you said..." or "I remember what you did last week." This pressing causes separation, because while you are pressing to hold them to yesterday, you also must press against yourself. And this can throw two of you out of balance.

Yesterday makes little difference to the process of NOW. At best, it can be a stepping-stone into the moment, but always and forever, you must let go of the past and move into the present and make this moment work for you.

23

People often come to me and say, "You know, two years ago you told me..." and I look at them and think, "So? You're not through that yet?" I tell them that there is no need for me to attempt clarification about what I said two years ago. If necessary, they can recall the information, bring it up to date, and make it work in this moment. But if they are still hanging on to an "answer" from two years ago, they are living in the past. They must bring it up to date, make it work right now, or forget about it. If you try to work out yesterday or last week or last year from the position of NOW, you can't do it, and you experience lack. Bring everything up to date, to this moment. Then in this moment you can work it or dismiss it and create all things new.

There are a lot of ways to dismiss the past. One way is to say, "I didn't know what was going on then." That doesn't excuse you from anything, but it may help take a little of the pressure off. Another way is to remember that from where you are in this moment, in this time and space, you are doing the best that you know to do. If you could do better in this moment, you would do better. If you are not doing so well, something is not allowing you to see completely your ability to do better. Something is blocking you. That doesn't excuse you, either, but it might allow you to be a little easier on yourself. Don't sit in judgment of your own lack of awareness or anyone else's. The action of judging demonstrates lack of awareness.

When you judge, you must label and pigeonhole. Then you nail the judgment down to make sure it will hold all the time. To do that, you have to extend yourself beyond your energy field, beyond your "**state of being**," and you are then in a state of upset and imbalance. When you extend beyond the limits of your awareness, you throw yourself off balance and must seek to get back to where you are anchored on this plane.

When you were born onto this earth, you received your

physical initiation. Nothing more was required to establish yourself here. You are here. You have empirical evidence; you have a body, and you have emotions and a mind. These are all elements of the earth, elements of the physical consciousness. These earthly elements are always due for change, so it behooves you to keep in the consciousness of change, in the consciousness of now, in the consciousness of the Spirit. Those things that you did yesterday are of yesterday. Today is a new day, and as you allow it, Spirit creates all things new for you each day.

To accomplish living in the NOW, you hold the emotions in an "up" consciousness, keep the mind focused on completion in the present moment, and keep the body healthy and able to hold the energy of Spirit. When you can do this, the consciousness expands to greater capabilities. Then comes the responsibility of holding your energies more in that greater field, and, of course, your reward is the ability to do more. Then your consciousness can expand to an even greater capability.

You become very competent with the ability to expand your consciousness and the responsibility to keep those energies flowing in the present. Then you move past the state of competence into the state of mastership, which encompasses all the levels from beginning to end, and still you must keep your energies flowing within the consciousness of NOW, which is both the beginning and the end as well as all moments between.

You can program yourself, suggest to yourself all the right and necessary and good things that you want manifest in yourself. You can do it at this moment, right now, with the energies you have present in the consciousness you are now expressing. You program what is right for you in this moment. If it changes tomorrow, then change to match it. There is nothing dishonorable about change. It is an aspect of Earth. You may not know what will happen tomorrow or a year from now or ten years from now. In this living eternity of time, you learn to make each decision based upon NOW, and if that changes, you flow with the change.

Sometimes decisions seem very hard to make because you don't want to make the wrong one. That is a negative approach. All decisions involve making a series of choices to move events around you from point to point within time and space. If you make a decision to go one way and it isn't working, then you make another decision to move in another direction. Ultimately, there are no right or wrong decisions; to decide as such is short-range vision. These are experiences of consciousness.

There are no catastrophes, only what appears to be catastrophes in the eye of the beholder. It is the wisdom of experience that you are gaining here on the earth plane, and then you transfer that wisdom from point to point in this world. If other people share their experiences with you and you learn from them, you can probably cut down the time you have to sit on the borders of fear and doubt and can more quickly discover the center of your beingness and reside in the presence and joy of Spirit. Finding the "state of being" can bring you a fulfillment and a joy greater than you have ever known on this earth. It transcends all the levels of mind, emotions, and body, and reaches to the inner Kingdom wherein resides all peace and joy and love.

Experiencing Spirit

Y ou are a child of God. You are a child of Light. The Soul that is your true identity resides naturally in love and joy. If you look to find the Beloved in all those around you, you will find the Beloved within yourself. If you see disturbance out there in the world, it is a reflection of disturbance in you. If you see something you don't like in another child of Light, it is because that same place exists inside of you, and you recognize that. All of your experiences, all of your relationships, reflect you back to yourself so that you can learn to know yourself in greater and greater ways. This life and all its experiences are for your upliftment and to assist you in your journey home to God.

A recycling process within each individual, continually allows the opportunity to experience all the laws of Spirit. You continually have a chance to check your expression as it is returned. The Spirit returns all things to you, as if to say, "Are you sure?" When you do what is best with what you know and where you are, and when you decide that whatever happens you will continue to lift yourself and use everything as an experience of consciousness, you will make it. You will endure all things, and you will find within yourself that "state of being" that is the blissfulness and the awareness of Spirit.

Man's consciousness is multidimensional. The physical is only a small part of the totality. Therefore, do not identify yourself exclusively as your physical body, your emotions or your thoughts. Those are tools to use for your learning; they are not your beingness. You learn with those things, and you know you have learned when you no longer repeat your errors.

People ask me if I ever become depressed. If I encompass all time and space, then the answer must be, "Yes." But if the question is whether I become depressed now, have been in the recent past, or anticipate having that feeling in the future, the answer is "No." Depression is only a way of looking at things that says there is lack or failure within the consciousness. It is demonstration that you have moved away from your "state of being" and have falsely identified with some level less than that of Spirit.

Long ago, I told myself that whenever that feeling of depression came in, it would immediately move me to joy. I reprogrammed depression for happiness. So if that feeling begins to come in, I start lifting immediately. Anything less than the "state of being" can be used to program you back into a "state of being." Anything off center can be used to move you back to center.

As you journey along the path of spiritual enlightenment, you may discover many, many misconceptions about the "spiritual person." The most basic factor of spiritual teachings is that **you are already spiritual**. There is nothing that you need to do to become that. There is no ritual you must perform to become spiritual. There are no books that you must read to become spiritual. There is no prescribed way you must behave to be spiritual. You **are** spiritual. You are a being of Spirit. It is your essence, your greatest reality.

You do not have to try to become spiritual. You don't have to try to be what you already are. The process of **trying** is like using a double negative; it's redundant. In a sense, **trying** to be spiritual is like a female trying to be female. She already is; it's not necessary to try. She might "try" to match her expression with some outer criteria or someone's opinion, but that she is a female is a fact. Men and women are spiritual beings. They do not have to **try** to

28

become that. To express that spirituality consciously in day-to-day activities may be a little bit different. They may have to work to express that quality more directly.

A spiritual master once said to me, "Do you remember the part of the great misunderstood book, the Holy Bible, which says, 'Take off your shoes because you stand on Holy ground'?" I said, "Oh yes, I recall this from early religious teachings. Do you think that passage means the particular mountainside where they stood was Holy ground?" He said, "Anywhere a man stands is Holy ground if he knows and can recognize his inner spiritual awareness. If he can be aware of the Christ action and the Holy Spirit within himself, he is indeed walking on Holy ground." When I thought about this, it made much more sense to me than to think just one spot was Holy ground and everything else was barren and unfruitful. I went back and checked the Bible and found it really didn't refer to **one** particular place as Holy ground, but that wherever spiritual men are, individually or collectively, is Holy ground.

What is a spiritual man or a spiritual woman? What should a person be doing who is manifesting Spirit? A few thousand years ago, Jesus walked on the water, and this was considered to be a spiritual action. However, if someone today were to walk on the water, people might clap and ask where the rocks were. Or they might check for the wires supporting him or say it wasn't really deep water and just looked deep. Or they might say the illusion was caused by mass hypnosis because everyone knows you can't walk on water. At times, ancient masters ascended and descended on pillars of fire and Light. If this were to happen now, people would probably clap and say, "That's a pretty good trick; what can you do for an encore?" Yet at that time, those things were recognized as having high spiritual attributes. And was it true? It was phenomena; that's for sure.

Does a spiritual person perform rituals? Does a

spiritual person walk around sprinkling holy water on everyone? Not necessarily, but they could. More likely than not, those rituals we traditionally think of as being indicative of Spirit more accurately reflect a religious approach. There is a difference between religious and spiritual. Spiritual people are rarely caught up in dogma or creed, but religious people have almost inevitably formed dogmatic processes in which they work. And that's okay. That's their expression; they have a right to express that way. They can do as they please; everybody can.

Spiritual people may put on saffron robes and trek through Tibet or India with a little wooden bowl, exchanging services for food. They may read letters or write letters for people as payment for food and shelter. This type of exchange *is* also a spiritual action. The spiritual person "pays" for what he receives. Today, for the most part, money is the spiritualized medium of exchange with which we work. It is spiritual. It is a convenient way in a complex society to exchange goods for services. So the spiritual person can live and work within modern, Western society.

The spiritual life *is* compatible with modern society. To realize the truth of that statement, just adjust your point of view to accommodate the realization that Spirit manifests in many, many ways; you'll find yourself in pretty good territory. If you can't widen your point of view, you'll find yourself in frustrations and "problems." Your inability to control your "problems" can bring despair. Then you start getting depressed and go down in your consciousness into feelings of, "Nobody loves me; nobody cares; woe is me; I'm no good." You go into these expressions because you feel you can't control what's going on in your environment.

You can control *yourself* (attitude) within your inner environment, but you cannot control your outer environment. The sun is coming up tomorrow whether you like it or not. You might say, "I know that; who would try to control that?" That's an extreme example, yes. But many times it is helpful to take things far out so that you can perceive more clearly that which is close. It would be just as useless for me to try to control the blood flowing through someone's body as to try to control the sun. I may tell it to stop, but it will keep right on going. You might think that's a little extreme, too. But in the same way, I can't control anyone's mind or emotions or opinions. I can't make people do anything by saying that people shouldn't do something **that** way or that they should do it **this** way. If they don't see it my way, they are certainly not going to do it my way. They are going to do it their way, and they have that right and that freedom.

Too many times you expect people to do what you think they are supposed to do. Then when they don't do it that way, you get upset. You've placed them on a pedestal. You've said, "You have to do it this way because I expect you to." That's not an enviable position to place anyone in or to be placed in. When people try to put me on a pedestal, I get right back off again because I just don't have time to keep my shoes shined their way. I'm too busy working. And when I'm working, I sometimes don't have time to do what another person wants or expects.

Don't try to control people. Just let them unfold the way they want. It's beautiful to sit with others and have them start telling you about themselves. The support is in listening and hearing them reveal themselves to you a little bit at a time while you remain free of judgments or preconceived opinions about what they should or shouldn't be. It can be much like reading a book; it's nice to read it one page at a time and get the quality of what it's about. If you are a speed reader, you will read it faster, and you can still get the quality of the book. Some people reveal themselves to you much more rapidly than others. And many times people reveal much more by what they don't say than by what they do say. You have to learn to read between the lines. If you can't, it's because you have prejudices. Your mind is thinking that it has to be a certain way. There are no "cer-

31

tain ways" on this planet. There are only ways that work and ways that don't work. And when people reveal themselves to you, they tell you about those things that either worked or didn't work for them.

Listen well when other people share with you. Their information is valuable. You can use others' lessons and experiences to supplement your own. You may be going through experiences similar to theirs and be able to learn from them which path to take. Or maybe you can use the information they give you to help someone else. If nothing else, their information may point up areas into which you do not wish to enter. Let each person be your teacher. You be the best student you can, and learn all you can from every situation. Then select those things that will work for you, **and work them**. Move ahead continually on the path of your own divine destiny. When you do this, you will be manifesting that which is spiritual, you will be expressing a quality of the spiritual person.

What determines whether you are more or less spiritually aware is your own individual ability to tune into the Spirit. The responsibility always comes back to you as an individual. There are many ways to have spiritual realizations and those things that come with spiritual realizations. You might think, "How can Joe be spiritual? He's a mechanic." Or "How can Harry be spiritual? He smokes three packs of cigarettes a day and sometimes doesn't shower." Those physical actions may have very little to do with being spiritual. Sometimes you say, "Look how spiritual Susie is. She goes to church every Sunday." But does she maintain that "Sunday consciousness" on Monday, Tuesday, Wednesday, Thursday, Friday and Saturday? A spiritual person may not necessarily be a church participant. They may be, but they are also in "church" the rest of the week. This is one key to the spiritual consciousness.

Another key is that the spiritual person is "on call"

twenty-four hours a day, "eight" days a week — on call when necessary, and sometimes on call even when not necessary. If nobody calls, that's fine. But the spiritual person is there if needed. Sometimes it's important to call if you need something, to communicate physically and verbally with people. When more communication is the only way to resolve something, the spiritual person is there to hold the Light and help you through the "rough spots." The consciousness spiritual people express is not to be **abused**, but it certainly is to be **used**. Often when you talk with a spiritual person, you can feel their Light and love and joy lifting you, giving you a clearer perception of your situation. Your enthusiasm builds as your consciousness lifts, and you go on your way refreshed and recharged.

The spiritual person is not necessarily free from the physical laws of the planet. The spiritual person does not disrupt spiritual laws that are being reflected through the physical laws of the planet. It's true that were you given the ability through God, you could create a universe. That power is there for you. But where would you put a universe? It's true that you could create all sorts of things in this physical world, but what would you do with them? Do you want to upset the plan that was instituted at the beginning of time? Not if you are expressing a spiritual consciousness. Rather, you come in line with what's going on and learn to **use** it to its highest potential.

Those who manifest their spiritual consciousness can be recognized by their ability to gain those things they move towards. Rarely can their progression be blocked. They will, however, be moving towards those things that are for their highest good, towards those things that lift them into greater spiritual awareness. If they go against that action, they find many blocks placed in front of them. They can, if they so desire, override the blocks, but it becomes difficult to handle. If you find yourself being blocked in your pursuit of a particular goal, you might be wise to step back, take another look at your action and your motivations, and reevaluate whether or not your goal is for your highest good and for the highest good of those people close to you.

The spiritual person **does** without expectation of reward, yet knows very well a reward is magnificent. The actions of service are completed with no sense of reward. And if a reward comes, it is taken care of with love, because the treasures have been laid up in Heaven. The spiritual person knows that all is right and proper and that everything is really going well, even when it may not appear to be that way. The spiritual person does not necessarily feel the negativity of this planet to any great extent, but maintains a consciousness open to the flow of the Light. As you open and let the spiritual love flow and direct your Light out into the world, you become an instrument of the Light, and you lift to an even greater expression of your spirituality. Remember, you are already spiritual. You can increase the expressed spirituality by bringing more loving into your actions. Then your expression begins to reflect more and more purely the spiritual being you are.

Spiritual progression is
a continual process of
leaving behind the old,
familiar patterns and
venturing into the new.
The whole trip can
become an adventure.

Spirit Is A Process Of Now

Chapter Two

Many realms of beingness exist simultaneously. Most people are readily aware of the physical realm and can identify it most easily. It is very evident: you have a physical body and are existing on this realm. There are other levels of which you may or may not be aware. Above the physical is the astral, which equates with the imaginative-emotive process within you. The "boogey men," the fears and the fantasies that you create have form and substance in the astral realm. The causal realm equates with your feelings and emotion, with the level of your feelings. The mental realm equates to the process of your mind. The etheric realm equates to your unconscious processes. And the Soul realm equates to the Soul, which is your beingness. The Soul is your truest reality. All lower levels are illusionary and transient.

The lower realms (etheric, mental, causal, astral, physical) are all created. They are complete. You are simply awakening to that creation in more complete and total ways all the time. Creation in the higher realms is active, dynamic, ongoing, in the process of becoming. Creation in the lower worlds **appears** to be ongoing because the process of awakening to it is ongoing and will be for a long, long time. But in about thirteen to fifteen billion years, the lower levels of creation as we now know them will be pulled back into God, and this that now exists will become void.

There are many opportunities to reach into your knowingness and discover that which is, thereby releasing yourself from the cycle of reincarnation and freeing yourself to move consciously into the higher realms and become part of the ongoing process of creation. You are at the threshold of your knowingness; now it's just a matter of moving into that knowingness. You are at the threshold of beingness; it's your choice when to move into that. You may stay on the threshold for many, many years. Or you may move into your knowingness right now. It's difficult to make that step into knowingness, into beingness, unless you are willing to commit totally to yourself, to the Soul that is YOU. And it is difficult to commit to that discovery if you split your energies into various pursuits and paths.

Those who are into the process of self-discovery, of Soul discovery, find that experiences on the various realms of Light become as real as physical realm experiences. As you come to trust your own experience level of realms different than the physical, you begin to experience the transcendence of the Soul.

The Soul extends into the lower realms in order to experience the totality of God. Its purpose is, in essence, to experience. For the evolution of the Soul, experiences do not need to be repeated because the purpose of each experience is fulfilled with the completion of that experience. When you begin to work with the Mystical Traveler Consciousness, you often find your progression greatly speeded up. You may find yourself moving through many experiences and just letting them go as they complete themselves. There is less and less need to hang onto the old, more and more excitement with discovering what's next.

If you attempt to move back into an experience of yesterday, even if that experience was pleasurable, you may find it gone. And if you persist in your attempt to recapture that, you experience frustration and, very often, pain and confusion. Many people encounter great difficulty in attempting to live somewhere other than **now**. Difficulty comes if people remember the past and the sweetness of it and then try to make it work for today. Difficulty also comes if people project out into the future and try to make it happen in a particular, preconceived way, or if they look forward in fear to what might occur. If you cut out the apprehension of the future and the memories of the past you are experiencing present. If you forget to remember, you can be here now.

Spirit is a process of **now**. Spirit only exists now. If you try to attach to the past or the future, you get stuck and may feel the absence of Spirit, because it cannot exist for you outside of **now**. That process of attachment to past or future can become a fixation within your consciousness.

If you experience a disappointment through some experience, that disappointment exists at the moment of its happening and is valid in that moment. But if you hang on to it and let it affect the next moment — and the next, and the next — it becomes a fixation and starts controlling you. Let it go and move into now. Nothing exists, in actuality, before or after the moment it happens. If you have a fight with your loved one and he or she says something that hurts you, the hurt exists in that moment and is valid in that moment. If you let those words color everything else from that moment on, the incident has become a fixation and will beat you up like you can't believe. Let each moment go as it happens. That's the road to freedom.

You can only break a fixation when it's present. Maybe you smoke cigarettes and would like to stop. You can't break the fixation of smoking when you don't feel the urge to smoke. The time to break the smoking habit is **not** after you've had a cigarette and are feeling balanced and happy. The best time to break the smoking habit is **when you want that next cigarette**. You can break the habit when you pick up the cigarette and start to light it. That's the time to throw it away. If you light it, you give in and are still controlled by your fixation. This same process applies to any fixation, whether it's drinking, over-eating, lust, or whatever.

You stop fixations of the past by not entering into reverie and memory of the past. You stop fixations of the future by not moving into fantasy and wishful thinking about what's coming up. You live now, entirely present and participating in each moment of your life, and your life just unfolds to you in the way that is right and proper for you. You find yourself experiencing happiness as you experience the spiritual flow that is present every moment.

One way to come into the moment is to move into meditation or prayer and hold your consciousness very, very steady. That enables you to move past the dominion of your fixations into freedom. Your prayer might be just counting to one hundred. If you are doing that as a tool to hold your mind and attention steady, it can work for you. If you tune inward to your Self as you count, you may discover many levels with yourself where you can break through many fixations.

One of the most difficult fixations is the expectation of what other people should do for you. It's called judging; sometimes it's called prejudice or pre-judging. If you burn your hand on the stove and hate all stoves from that point on, that's prejudice. Silly? Yes, but people apply that same logic to interpersonal relationships. The process is just as invalid, regardless of what it's applied to. If you enter into an **evaluation** of the situation, you may decide that putting your hand on the stove allows it to get burned. It doesn't make the stove "bad" or "against you." It's just an evaluation of what is, and you can work with that. That's easy. If you move into fear, expectation or fixation, you're going to have some difficulty.

Living here and now is freedom. Spirit will never give you anything you can't handle. So you can be assured that you will always be able to handle what is. You do that by staying present in the moment and just moving through each experience as it appears. Those of you who work with the Mystical Traveler consciousness know that I go through these things with you. You are never alone. You are perfectly protected at all times. And as you become aware and trusting of that process, life can become very joyful.

Lifting Beyond "Problems"

I t is possible for you to lift out of your present level of consciousness into other, higher levels of consciousness. This can be challenging, though, if you have not considered the possibility before. Often you must have a key given to you, a door pointed out, a keyhole or a doorknob brought to your attention. Then it is up to you to take action. If you don't do anything, then you sit with the keys, the information, the knowledge and the where-with-all to change your life. But nothing will happen unless you do it. Let's look at the factor of ''not doing'' for a moment.

You may often find yourself making decisions by default. This is when you won't make a decision ''for'' or ''against'' and then find a decision forced upon you from outside of yourself. You may not be too happy about that type of decision, but if you will not take action, action will be forced upon you. Too often you become hesitant about making a wrong decision — if any decision can be called ''wrong.'' In reality, there are no wrong decisions. Through all my experience of working with people in both this level and other levels of consciousness, I have found that there is no wrong decision except as people label it ''wrong.''

After you have decided on something, you can look at that decision, that movement or direction, as a lesson, simply a lesson, a problem-solving technique. If it solves the problem, then you are content with the decision. If it does not, you make another decision. Whichever way your decision leads you, it is a positive action because it promotes direction and forward movement.

When you can't see your way out of a problem, when you can't see a direction, when you can't make a decision, that's when you feel "boxed in" or at the mercy of the circumstances. And this brings in frustration and a feeling of incapability. A lot of people get stuck in this and label it an "inferiority complex." One man said to me, "I have an inferiority complex." I said, "Maybe it isn't a complex!" He looked at that idea for a while and said, "Maybe it's not." I said, "Is it possible that in that particular area, you **are** inferior?" He thought about that and said, "Yes, I believe I am." I said, "Then why don't you work in an area where you are not inferior?" He worked through that for awhile and decided that he would be better suited to another area. He moved to the new area and experienced much greater success. Then he worked on the weak area in his spare time until it was stronger also. In other words, he accurately evaluated where his strengths were, utilized his strengths to their fullest potential, and worked on the weak areas to build them into strengths that could also be used to enhance his expression.

Too many times the "problem" is allowing a situation to come to you on the level of your weakness and then declaring it too much for you to handle. Then it represents a **problem**. It's only a problem as far as you see it that way; someone else may look at it and perceive the solution immediately. Many times what you are looking at as a problem isn't a problem at all, but an expression. When you perceive it as an expression and see that there are many alternative ways to express, you have a way to move through it and change it to another expression.

If you look at life as being a ladder, you can visualize each "problem" as a rung in that ladder. If you take away the problem, you may take away your potential growth. You learn from your experiences, and often you learn more from your negative experiences than your positive experiences. Those experiences that hit at you and shake you are often most effective areas of learning.

43

You all know the good times you've had. Look at all the time you've wasted trying to have a good time. And what did you really accomplish? Didn't the good times appear spontaneously? Didn't they just appear in the course of your living? You moved through them very fluidly and joyfully. How about the bad times? Can't you almost remember who said what to whom and what the whole situation was about? Can't you feel the hurt and the turmoil in your stomach? Yes, because you may be learning and remembering more through the negative process. But if you can use that negative process as a stepping-stone, then has it really been negative? You have turned it into a positive action. You surmount negativity by standing on the things that appear to be negative and using them to lift you higher. The "problem" is still there; you just shift your consciousness in relation to it and start rising above it and discovering that YOU are greater than any "problem" and that YOU have the keys to solve all "problems."

As soon as you realize there is an answer to every problem, it becomes easier to find the answer. Sometimes the answer is to do nothing, to hold steady, to make the decision not to move. A lot of times people get caught up in the need for action. They say, "I have to do something about this!" If asked why, they might say, "Because I just have to!" And that's not necessarily a good answer. You might ask, "What if you do this?" They say, "That won't work." You say, "Okay, what if you do this?" They say, "That won't work either." So you say, "What if you just hold still?" Maybe they're a little more receptive to that idea now. So they hold still, and that stillness allows the solution to come into their mind. They see their direction and are on their way. Then they say, "Thank God I didn't do anything rash. It's a good thing I didn't make up my mind impetuously."

Sometimes "decison by default" can be a good approach, and most of the time, because you are a directive force and energy in motion, it's best to have conscious,

44

directed movement. It is your building action. It is your growth. As soon as you have declared an intent one way or the other, you put your energy into that decision. Then if it does not feel clear, you can reverse your decision and direct the energy another way. If you don't direct yourself, if you spend your time on a "tightrope," you usually end up frustrated. It's often necessary to make a movement. In such a situation, any decision you make, any direction you move, can be for your highest good, no matter what it is. The important thing is that you can move forward, move up, and in that process of moving, you develop many self-correcting devices. You can constantly evaluate and change your direction, your movement, your decisions. One decision does not lock you in. And as you keep moving, nothing can stop you from moving your consciousness into higher and higher levels of awareness.

Dealing With Dilemmas

I t has often been said that it takes great courage to see the face of God. And this is true because you must see past all the illusions of the lower levels to see the face of God. You must see past the conditioning of this world and this society. You must see past the illusion of your own senses. You must see past your own dilemmas. God is present in everything. God is entirely present, all the time. Your dilemma is your misunderstanding of the absolute "hereness" and "nowness" of God's presence. And in your misunderstanding, you give yourself over to negative power, to the dilemma.

The problem appears when you separate "here" and "there," when you perceive yourself as being "here" and someone or something else as being "there." Then you want those other people or things, and you reach out to touch them and find you can't. You start to master the situation only when you go beyond the dilemma. If you only sit "here" and perceive the situation "there," you think it's overwhelming. So you "die." That's the problem. Yet the part of you which becomes overwhelmed **should** die. It should always be confronted. It should be presented with continual confrontation, but not in resistance.

Resistance is another problem. You can never confront and **win** with resistance. To win, you confront each situation by slowly expanding your energy field, your ego field, and reaching out to meet and encompass the new situation. If you just meet each situation, one at a time, it's very easy. As soon as you feel like, "Oh, I'm blowing it; it's falling on my head," pull your energy field back in and shore it back up again; hold steady. Maybe you hold steady for a month, just holding your balance, looking at the situation, thinking, "Why does it think it can outlast me? While it is in a state of change, I can be in a state of spiritual holding and fulfillment and outlast the change."

That inquiry and that realization throws you right back into the center, into Spirit and Soul. When you come back and find the center, the spiritual energy starts radiating out. But now it does not radiate out as a personality or as an expression of the physical senses, but from the center of lightness which is your own Light. It radiates out and becomes the order of your universe. Then there is nothing you cannot do because everything takes on an equal quality. If someone spilled a bag of precious jewels, you'd pick them up and put them back. If someone spilled a load of fresh manure on the road, you'd shovel it back. They're both the same.

Your strength resides in the spiritual consciousness. It can never reside outside yourself in a form. Because it is physical, a form is always corruptible. That's why you rarely have your or anyone else's spiritual form revealed to you. You or someone else might attempt to destroy it. It's much like the old saying that those who live by the sword, die by the sword. Those who live by the form, die by the form. As that form destroys, it will be destroyed, not necessarily by sword or spear, but by some form which fulfills that destruction. Everyone has heard of someone who has killed another person and lived without any apparent repercussions. But perhaps the person "died" by another form, which could have been an agony or suffering greater than a physical death would have brought about. Perhaps the form that "killed" the person was that of a young lover who would not have anything to do with him. Perhaps it was another form that had within it the potential for destruction.

If you are in a position of being destroyed by a form, by a situation that you seem unable to control, that's your dilemma. If a young man is being rejected by the girl he desires, his first step in resolving the dilemma could be the understanding of, "Wow, I can't have her. That's my dilemma. That's my karmic flow right now. So since I can't have her, I'm just going to do what I can do."

Many times, however, the image of that girl will continue to reappear in his mind, and it will be very difficult for him to keep himself in balance. If he allows that image to stay, if he masturbates with her in his mind, if he puts energy with that image, he is creating and perpetuating his dilemma. He's putting everything into an image that has nothing to do with his present involvement. The way to change the situation is to insert, at the time of the greatest energy, at the time of climax, a new image and move the sexual energy into that new image. Soon he will no longer feel the great desire for her. That's one way to handle the dilemma. The image now takes the energy and moves into another framework, according to your understanding. The faster you can understand your dilemma, either by being told, by reading, by being confronted, by direct experience, or by anything else, the faster you can immediately turn from and pass on the learning, the training, and the experience to the next person. Then there is an immediate change which is the upward flow of energy.

These dilemmas that you create for yourself can be changed, can be understood and dissolved. But you have to be eternally watchful and alert. You just don't sit and watch a rock fall on your head. You have to be smart enough to see the rock, move, get out of its way when it falls so that there's no dilemma of, "What do I do with a broken leg?" Some people expect the rock to fall, and their expectation creates it; it falls on them, and they say, "Why me?" — Why not? They set it there, they diagrammed it, they created it and pulled it to them, and it broke their leg. That dilemma is over, unless they re-create it and let a rock fall on the other leg. Skiers and drivers who are accident prone have a similar dilemma of creating accidents by expecting them. Whether it's wrecking the car, falling on skis, knocking over glasses of water, stubbing toes, whatever — it's all the same underlying dilemma. It's hidden and calloused over and it's sometimes so deep that the only way to get to it is through the psychoanalytical process.

Before you involve yourself in psychotherapy, you have to get through the dilemma that blocks you from going to the psychiatrist. Most people's dilemma is so powerfully ingrained that they'll say, "A psychiatrist can't help me. Those guys need help themselves. What good are psychologists and psychiatrists? How are they going to find out what's going on inside of me when I don't have any way of knowing myself?" The psychologists and psychiatrists can help you simply because they are not part of your dilemma.

You may go to a psychiatrist and see his dilemma and think, "Gee, he should get on his own couch." If you've gone to him to criticize and judge him, you've lost. The psychiatrist may see your dilemma and say, "Well, that goes back to early childhood." Then he starts the process of chopping out the old blocks and dilemmas. That process can be so painful that you want to get up and run away, and you call the psychiatrist every name you can think of. He sits there, knowing that all the fear, the striking out and the cursing are part of the manifestation of the dilemma. He says, "I expect this to take place in those people who come to me because I'm sort of the last resort." As he continues breaking loose the blocks of consciousness, he may penetrate the core and release the dilemma. Yet, unless you have something ongoing to support the change, like a religious philosophy or a way of life, your dilemma will regrow again.

The progression and regression in dealing with dilemmas often follows a typical pattern in psychoanalysis. The first year you really do well, making lots of progress by breaking through the blocks and dissolving the dilemmas. The second year you do even better; things really become

49

clear. The third year, because you aren't changing your life pattern, your environment, your philosophy or your approach, the dilemma takes over again. And as the psychiatrist starts to come into that area again, to break it free, you put up great resistance and say, "What a waste! Three years in psychoanalysis, and I'm no better off than before." The dilemma reaches up again more strongly than ever, and you deny all future help, even God's. And that's really serious, serious trouble.

When you understand the dilemma of the heart, change it, dissolve it, clear it and then reevaluate and rebuild a new base where things are born clear again. It's true that a new dilemma or a similar one may come up almost immediately, but you learn the process of confronting, dissolving and clearing each one, and you continually apply it to each new dilemma that appears. You continually reevaluate and rebuild. You recognize that your strength is in the spiritual consciousness, in the spiritual form which cannot be perceived with physical senses, and more and more you move to that. You place your direction and your desires there. Then you win your freedom over the dilemmas.

Overcoming Dilemmas

That which is called the human consciousness is in a constant state of change and, if you will, of decay and rebirth. As the consciousness moves higher and higher, you leave behind the old familiar patterns; you let them go and continually move into new areas. This can be a frightening experience and difficult to handle if you don't know where you're going. Let's create an analogy: suppose you are in a car, riding with some acquaintances, and you don't know where they are taking you. You could become worried or concerned or frightened. If you started up into a wilderness area, you might begin to feel as if you were going to be hurt or harmed in some way. You might think you were going to be dropped off and left there, or you might become fearful of being killed. If one of your companions asked why you were creating those types of fears, you might say, "I have good reason to create that; I saw that very thing in a movie once." Your companion might reply, "There's nothing to worry about. Just hang on; when we get to the end, you'll find out for yourself." You might say, "No, I can't just hang on. I have to know what's going to happen." And your dilemma of "having to know" would perpetuate itself and block you from experiencing each moment for itself. As you create expectations of people or of situations, as you create opinions of what should or should not be taking place with you and with others, you create your dilemmas.

A man may become an alcoholic because he cannot live up to his parent's, his spouse's, or his own expectations of himself — or what he imagines those expectations to be. He may drink because whatever he thought should be happening isn't. There are a lot of reasons, and most of

51

them originate in the area of false expectations. Maybe he drinks because he feels he isn't being properly recognized or appreciated. It is not the drinking that is the dilemma. The drinking gives the person the feeling of getting out of the dilemma. It is the cause behind the drinking that is the underlying dilemma.

Part of the dilemma of the gunslingers of the Old West was that, through their actions, they created an expectation within other people of their behavior, and then that expectation cycled back to them and perpetuated itself. When they came into a new town, they weren't sure of how they would be accepted. Not knowing what their reception would be, they came in shooting. The message of their actions went out and produced more dilemma by producing more expectations of violence. What the gunslingers really wanted was to be sheriff and wipe out all the bad men, but instead they became the bad men trying to wipe out the sheriff. They were miserable — always on the run, always suffering, always seeking to get free of the law. Yet the familiarity of the past was always riding with them, tormenting them. When they rode into a new town, the familiar pattern was to rob the bank, rape the women, kill the sheriff and run.

There is an interesting dilemma created in situations of war. It is the dilemma of allowing someone else to make your decisions for you with the expectation that you will obey, no matter what. There are documented and publicized incidents where a man carried out the orders of his commander and was later court-martialed for that action. Having created the idea of obedience without question, the "powers that be" suddenly expect disobedience if an order is judged to be a bad one. The two points of view are in opposition. The new consciousness of people may be saying, "No, we're going to end that dilemma and challenge every order to see if it is right or wrong, to see the upliftment from the dilemma and move toward that." Then the dilemma involved in obedience without question can be alleviated. But those for whom that dilemma has already been created may find themselves being tried for committing an atrocity which before would have been looked at as nothing more than an "act of war."

It is even more interesting that many people for whom the dilemma involving obedience without question has already been created come home after the wars and go into local, state and national government. And they take the same dilemma with them — you do what you're told, no matter what. The dilemma is passed on in the form of regimentation versus the self-discipline of knowing what to do, of knowing what will uplift and following their own form of knowing so that they are free within their own direction and consciousness.

Even after the consciousness has recognized and identified a dilemma, it can be difficult to break through. Perhaps the hardest area to work with in overcoming a dilemma involves the cell memory level, because a dilemma that has become part of the cell memory can take between seven and eleven years to change, if you don't "backslide" or falter during that time. As soon as you falter, you start adding time.

One way to break a habit is to repeat a new pattern thirty-two times without faltering. As soon as you falter, you start again at one, but now it's necessary to repeat the new pattern more than thirty-two times; it may be forty-seven. It becomes difficult. At some point you may falter so much that you say, "What difference does it make anyway? I can't do it." So you give up and leave that whole area. And the dilemma is solved! As you stop placing energy and concern there, the dilemma drops away.

If a dilemma is strong, it may just transfer itself to another area. You leave one job for another job, and you feel really good about it. But it may be an artificial high, because the new job is simply more of the same — more games, more illusions, more words. You're feeding your-self the same old stuff, and you eat it because you think it's new. You eat it as fast as you can to make it ever more familiar, which is your dilemma.

Dilemmas are part of the negative power of the planet. They are part of the maya of the planet. We really don't need glamour and illusion and karma; just the general maya of the planet is enough. But man corrupted the lower levels by placing forth the glamour, the illusions and the personal karma of his own making, and then cemented the whole thing together so that the pollution isn't only in the physical environment, but within the physical body, the emotions, the mind, the unconscious and the psycho-spiri-tuality. Pollution is not in the Soul. The Soul is pure; it always has been and it always will be. It is within the other levels of consciousness that pollution occurs. And it is within the lower levels of consciousness that dilemmas occur.

When you get the vision of freedom as your goal, you can really start breaking through your dilemmas. As long as you don't know where you're going, you may break the immediate thing that is causing you pain without breaking the underlying dilemma. As soon as you can break through the underlying dilemma, all the others will start collapsing. Even if there are a lot of dilemmas to come, they'll be easier to handle once that first big one is completely broken. All you really have to do is handle each one as it comes into your consciousness. If you try to rush into them, you might create more dilemmas. Don't seek them. Just let them come to you naturally, if they will.

You're never given anything you can't handle — that's a spiritual dictum. As a new dilemma presents itself, you have the strength to handle it. There's never a loss. As soon as you have strength you can't use, it becomes a dilemma of what to do with your strength, your talent, your ability. Then the dilemma of frustration is upon you. **You** can handle all situations and overcome your dilemmas by moving to your center and pulling forward a universal strength. As soon as you move out to your periphery, you lose awareness of that center and that strength. You become confused and unsure and ask, "What should I do?" You think maybe you should do this, or maybe you should do that.....and there begins a dilemma. It is not necessary. Hold to your center. Maintain your center. Use everything that comes to you as grace. You'll build your strength that way.

As long as you keep your consciousness centered, as long as you keep yourself free of expectations, of opinions of what should or should not be taking place, and as long as you let your experiences flow into you, you are lifting. At that point, no matter who you are with or where you are, you will be moving forward on your path.

Moving Beyond
The Dilemmas

Lack of familiarity in a new situation can be the cause of a dilemma. Imagine a caveman in a modern kitchen; he's very, very thirsty, so that whether or not he can find water becomes a matter of life and death. In the kitchen is a sink with faucets which could provide clear running water if he were aware of how to turn them on. But the caveman doesn't know about that. He just knows he is in a strange, unfamiliar situation, dying of thirst, and he must get water.

A modern-day man, who would like to extend his help to the caveman, sits very helpless in the midst of plenty because the caveman, in his fear, will not let him in the kitchen. Anytime the man starts into the kitchen, the caveman takes his club and beats at him until he leaves. The man is not after the caveman's club; he just wants to help. So he goes back outside and dresses up like a caveman and comes back into the kitchen and grunts and groans and makes familiar sounds so the caveman can feel familiar and a little more secure. Then slowly he starts **toward the sink and the faucets, toward those things unfamiliar to the caveman — and it's likely the caveman** will hit him on the head and kill him because he is not following the behavior pattern that the caveman thinks is appropriate. After all, the caveman reasons all cavemen should be very afraid in this new situation and should be acting in a certain conditioned way.

If someone behaves differently, they're dangerous and should be killed. This is an age-old dilemma that man continually perpetrates against himself, individually and collectively. If you can keep your consciousness open and flowing and aware of all possibilities and potentials, if you can prevent yourself from falling into the trap of thinking that your way is the only way, you will certainly be further ahead.

Suppose in his search to find security, the caveman finds a fifty-gallon bucket of water, and he knows by rationing the water he can exist for four or five months. He feels very secure and safe. But four or five months go by quickly, and the water supply is seen as a very temporary situation. He had the most security when the bucket was full, and then he started falling from that point. What does he do when the water becomes low? He probably starts seeking for more water, for another water supply. It is that repeated seeking which can become a frustration.

At some point, we all recognize that there is water in the kitchen tap and that we simply have to turn it on; we realize that water is entirely present, at any moment, and that we do not have to go out looking for it. Some people will fill up the fifty-gallon bucket, anyway, and carry it around with them, just because that is a familiar, secure way to do it. After many years of watching other people get water out of the tap, they may get the idea that this other way seems to be working pretty well for a lot of people, so they put down their burden and go get water out of the tap, also, and discover that it does work pretty well. And then they feel a great pressure lift from them, and they feel a great sense of freedom.

There is a story of a man in the desert who had gone for many days without water and was becoming desperate for it when he saw an oasis in the distance. He walked toward it for many hours. When he was getting close, some other men came from another direction toward him. He was afraid that they were coming to steal "his" water, and he turned to fight them. As they came closer, they offered him water from the containers they carried. He accused them of being false and deceivers and of trying to beat him to the oasis to take ''his'' water. They tried again, explaining that they were only offering him water, but as they came up to him, he began to attack them. They finally persuaded him to turn toward ''his'' oasis and then asked, ''Tell us, what are you defending?'' When he looked again, the oasis was gone; it had been a mirage, a false image that he had been defending with his life. We often do these things. We fight and defend that which is false, that which is unreal, that which is not ours and never can be.

Dilemmas can appear whenever the human consciousness establishes an identification with something which is a false image. Suppose a girl goes to a movie and observes images of a romantic encounter. If she does not hold her consciousness neutral, in the role of the observer, she may find herself getting involved in the level the film is expressing. Then she may leave the movie and want to experience a romantic encounter. Perhaps her lifestyle at the present moment does not include that possibility or probability. So she may suddenly find herself entering into areas of consciousness and expression that are unusual.

Through her identification with the action of the movie, she has created a dilemma of desire within herself, and she will go out seeking to fulfill that dilemma. If she is successful in finding someone with whom to have a romantic encounter, it may not fulfill her anyway, because she is identifying with a false image which is unlikely to be matched in reality. And if she does not find anyone, she may go back to see another movie. Either way, she is perpetuating her dilemma. She may continue this pattern until she realizes it is not her reality she is chasing around attempting to fulfill, but the false image someone else has created for profit. With that awareness can come greater freedom.

A person may go to a movie and observe a scene of sexual deviation. And again, instead of maintaining his role of observer, he may identify with the movie so heavily that it causes him to fall out of his own consciousness of self and lose track of where he is going and what he is there for. If you go to the movies for diversion, for entertainment, that can be fine. But if you get all wrapped up in the movies to the point that you lose your own identity, you can leave with a dilemma.

Suppose the fellow who observes the scene dealing with deviation is married and has a son. The movie disturbs him so much that he has nightmares about his son becoming involved in that type of deviation. He finds that during the day he thinks about it, and there is horror within him at even the thought. That ''horror'' is a charge of energy that is placed with the thought. The son may pick up the father's dilemma, may become aware inwardly of his father's thoughts and fears and the energy patterns that are being placed out toward him. He may develop a complex which will affect his sexual attitudes, approach, and performance.

The son's dilemma becomes the fact that he goes from girl to girl to girl; and the dilemma hides itself because it is not his, even though he is part of it. If he could have a satisfying sexual experience with one woman and realize that there was very little chance of ever being corrupted, he could free himself; the dilemma would dissolve, and he'd be happy. Then, if his father began again to talk about sexual deviation, he could say, ''Dad, have you ever been corrupted?'' And when the father said, ''no,'' the son might say, ''Then why don't you just forget about it?'' The son may be able to forget about it, but if the father has perpetrated this thought over many years, he may find it very difficult to forget. This is a way that ignorance and, if you will, sin is perpetrated upon the child through the father's consciousness. It's an interesting process.

The fact that ignorance can be perpetrated in this way does not mean you should blame your parents for your dilemmas. For the most part, dilemmas are self-created.

Even if instigated by someone else, it is **you** who allows the dilemma to take control of your consciousness. Through awareness and understanding, all dilemmas can be dissolved. There is nothing that can bind you unless you allow it within your consciousness. Everyone has the potential of freedom within his or her own consciousness.

When you're traveling across the country in a car, you are in a state of constant change. You don't have to get out of balance, upset or disturbed because the scenery is changing. Similarly, parts of your life pattern will always be in a state of change. That's just the way it's set up. You don't have to get out of balance when things change for you.

As you're traveling across country, you may modify your responses as you come into new territory. When you get up into the Colorado Rockies, you may wear heavier clothing because it may be cooler. In the high altitude, you won't get out and run up a hill very fast. You'll go a little slower and take care of yourself. If you remember how fast you could run in the mountains at age eighteen and then try to do that at age forty-five, you have a dilemma going. This is the dilemma of a lot of "weekend athletes." They remember the athletic ability of eighteen and try to duplicate it, and they end up with physical difficulties. Other middle-aged men who were good athletes when they were young try to live off past glories, continually talking about their past accomplishments, which tend to become "greater" as the years go by. Either approach can be a dilemma. The best approach is simply to live in the now, do the best you can with present abilities and talents and let your actions speak for themselves. That takes understanding. That takes awareness. It also takes love and respect for self. With it comes freedom, a sense of self-worth and an inner security and serenity that is worth everything. The only permanent solution to any dilemma is God. And God already IS.

Spiritual progression is a continual process of leaving behind the old, familiar patterns and venturing into the new. When you're working with a spiritual teacher, you'll feel that it's like taking a trip with a good friend whom you trust and who knows the road. Then the whole trip can become an **ADVENTURE** because you know where you're going and how to get there. There is no dilemma except as you create it. When you work with the Mystical Traveler, you might ask yourself if you place your dilemma between you and the Mystical Traveler and the love that is present. Once you tune to the Mystical Traveler and his love, all dilemmas disappear and strength is present.

When you start
exploring the inner
Spirit that allows each
person to exist as a
special individual, you
start finding a treasure
chest of love.

Discover Loving

Chapter Three

A s the Mystical Traveler, the work that I do is rarely of the physical plane. It is of the spiritual level. Many people, when they hear of spiritual things, mistake the quality of a spiritual life with being "kooky" when, in the greater reality, it is the only natural thing there is. Everything else could be considered the "kooky" area. The only qualities that endure are the spiritual qualities. All other qualities dissolve and disappear.

When you start exploring the inner consciousness, the inner Spirit that allows each person to exist as a special individual, you start finding a treasure chest of love, understanding, faith, hope, charity....and wishful thinking, superstition, gossip, war-mongering and lust. Those are all parts of the treasure chest. And all of it is precious. All of it. If you took a diamond out of the ground and looked at it in its rough form, chances are you would not know that it was a diamond. If, however, it were polished and the facets delineated, you would be able to tell that it was a diamond. Yet, you might throw a rough diamond away as being a dirty old nothing, while inside it is very beautiful and valuable.

Have you ever thought about the value of jealousy? Have you ever considered that quality, like most negative qualities, could be a diamond in the rough? Jealousy says, "I really care about you. I **really** care. I care so much it makes me sick. I care so much I can't even live my own life. When you reach that point of emotional involvement and investment in another person, jealousy enters. You have so much of yourself wrapped up with the other person that he, or she, has to live life your way or you just can't stand it.

Jealousy can really be beautiful. Wouldn't you like it if God came down and said, "I am so jealous of you, I care so much that I'm going to help you live your life more perfectly than ever before"? You might prefer to live your life yourself, in the best and clearest way you know how. You might say, "Lord, would you mind leaving my life to me? I don't want a jealous God. I want one that will let me do it my way." A jealous God might say, "Not on your life. You do it **my** way. And if you don't, just wait and see what happens to you." God doesn't do that. God continually presents to you the keys for discovering within yourself the ways that work for you.

You can't live a life of jealousy for very long, but you can use those qualities of jealousy to lift you. A long, long time ago, I was working with a very beautiful Master. I wasn't too dumb, but I certainly wasn't the smartest one in the class, either. This great Master promoted somebody else, and quite a few of us didn't like that at all. We thought that any Master worth his salt would know that we were the "chosen" ones, or he wouldn't be the Master. Any Master should know that, even the "dummy" we were following.

The reality was that we were sitting on the fringe of the class, on the outskirts of what was. We were actually getting ready to miss the boat entirely. We were creating our own return trip, our own failure. The Master had told us of our divinity, but how could we trust him? Look at who he promoted! I mean, these guys who were following all the rules and doing everything just right — they didn't know any more than we did. We asked them questions, and they were pretty nice, but they didn't tell us any answers. We became very jealous of their success, and we raised a lot of hell.

God bless our Master. He was so smart that he used our jealousy to get us back into the class where we belonged. When we had nothing else going for us except absolute bigotry, prejudice, jealousy, envy, hate, and even a little lust, he called us together and said, "If you want the success the others have, why don't you work for it?" It had never really occurred to us we had to work for a desired position. It had never occurred to us these things had to be earned. We took it for granted that when the class graduated, we would graduate. We found out we were so busy complaining and getting involved in petty areas that we weren't graduating. We had been there a long time. New students were coming and graduating, and we were still there.

Eventually something started awakening inside. We suddenly realized we had been there for a very long time and still weren't getting it. The Master used the jealousy and envy to make us get down and dig. Then we started getting it. When you have delayed and dragged your anchor for a long time, thinking you have been at safe harbor rather than lost at sea, you get to come back and experience that again. So we had to come back, and guess who the Master was? One of the "dummies" who had been our classmate previously. He said, "I remember you. I was with you before. You're doing the same routine now that you did before." Something inside said, "You're right. I know you are right. I don't exactly know the details, but I'm not going to repeat the same mistakes." The Master said, "Now, the way to break this is to do these particular things. You can do them your own way, but do them. They will break open these patterns and free you. It won't be easy. If it were easy you would have already done it, and you wouldn't be back here." I said, "Right, I acknowledge being the 'dummy' here. I acknowledge where I am, and I will work from that position."

It is often from the consciousness of "know-it-all" that you voice your answers, not realizing that it isn't necessary to know the answer to every question. It is only necessary to know how to get into the Soul body, traverse your own inner realms, then the outer realms, and establish yourself in the Soul realm. Then when you drop the physical body, you can go right home. Only that is necessary. All the rest is tiddlywinks, fun and games, and heartache. I don't care to play in a lot of those areas, so I don't. That is why I say that I will work with you in my own way.

Some people are really surprised that I have a way that works. It does work, and I am very happy to share it with you. But I will not do it your way. **You** do it your way. I found the way that works for me, and as long as you allow me to work my way with you, I modify it in the inner consciousness in a way that will work for you, too. Those who are established as my votaries, those with whom I work, are often not even aware when I am present within, working. They seldom perceive that things are changing unless it is necessary to let them know, to establish a rapport in their consciousness. Then they will see a purple flash of color or a purple ball or hear a whoosh that is awfully hard to miss. Sometimes they will hear me laugh from very deep within and know my presence.

Whatever your way is, do yourself a favor and use that way. No matter what comes into your consciousness, whether you call it evil or imbalance or anything else, use it to lift you. Make it part of what works for you. Can you use depression to get into the Soul consciousness? Can you use anger to Soul travel? Yes, by using it to identify another way that doesn't work. It's pretty simple. As you identify and eliminate what doesn't work, you come closer and closer to what **does** work.

People ask me if I get depressed. I don't, but I know that feeling. I look at it as something that is occasionally worn, but can be taken off and laid aside when no longer needed. I don't identify myself as depressed. I can take off a shirt and wear a different one. Depression works the same way. You can put it on and wear it, then take it off. But if you say you **are** depressed, by your own spiritual law, you lock yourself in. So you become depressed. If you say, "I am having a bad time," believe me, my friend, you are either having a bad time or certainly will be in a short time. Your own spiritual law will institute it for you.

Depression, the feeling of not being worthy and not being able to handle your life, can become very familiar. Even though you don't like it, you play the game that pulls it to you because it is a familiar game. Then you remain depressed, thinking, "Now I know who I am; I am nothing." A little voice inside says that you must be **something**, because look at how you can criticize. You criticize people from yourself, so you must be something. So why, then, do you go around saying that you are nothing? Your answer might be, "Well, I know that I am something, but I **feel** like I am nothing." That makes a little more sense. A lot of times, you may feel inadequate, based upon a certain situation. But it's certainly not necessary to allow that feeling to control your life.

If you happened to be in some foreign land where the natives, who still fought with spears, were coming at you, and if you had a magic carpet that could zip you away instantly — what would you do? I'll bet you would get out of there — **fast!** I doubt you would say, "Magic carpet, would you please take me up into the air." I think you would probably have that carpet keyed to one word: **"UP."** Yet people walk into situations like depressions and won't say "up" at all. They stand there and let the natives "throw spears" at them. Then they say, "Isn't it great how I'm handling this?"

If you don't feel equipped to handle something, tell people that. Tell them, "I just can't handle that." That is so real and so simple. If you have trouble seeing how that works, think of having an ingrown toenail and having someone in hiking boots step on your foot. I'm sure you would say, "HEY, GET OFF MY FOOT. IT HURTS!" They'd get off and say, "I'm sorry. I didn't know. Take care of yourself." When you honestly tell people you are not equipped to handle what they are laying on you, they can act in cooperation and, often, in loving concern.

When you see another person get badly hurt, you're usually anxious to assist that person. If necessary, you get them in the car and rush them to the hospital. You chance getting speeding tickets. If people get in your way, you move them aside and say, "Get out of my way. I have to get this person help. I'm not concerned about me. Pick on me later. Right now, I am helping this person." You do it, and when you get all through, you're so weary you could cry. But there is a feeling inside of you that says, "Well done." You sigh, "God, I feel good. I'm exhausted. I'm going to go home and collapse." And you do. Sometimes you even dream about the situation because you are still involved in it. Sometimes you just drop off into a very deep sleep and wake up feeling very good because you were given the opportunity to assist another bearer of Light and you fulfilled that. You rushed in and assisted a person who was incapable of assisting himself. In such a situation, the response must be appropriate to the situation, however. If someone cuts his or her finger a little and you rush them to the emergency room of the hospital, that response may not be appropriate; perhaps only a bandaid was needed.

When you feel like you can't handle a situation, it's often because you're afraid to attempt it. And often when you're afraid to attempt it, it's because you're afraid to make a mistake. Lean into what seems to be the right action and see what happens. Check the feeling you get inside. Put the Light with it. If it balks on you, let it go. If it seems to be flowing, flow with it — not with what you think **should** be taking place, unless it matches with what **is** taking place. Move out of the consciousness of mistakes and into the consciousness of experiencing.

Giving And Receiving

L ife is an ongoing experience. Have you ever done something really right, and within it, made a mistake? Sure, then you hurry and get the mistake cleared up so nobody knows about it. That's okay. Many years ago, I was visiting the home of an older lady who was a very dear friend of mine. I asked her to make some of her special homemade bread. So she made the bread for me, and when it was ready, I cut it, buttered it, took a bite — and oh, God, it was terrible. She had forgotten the salt. Have you ever tasted bread without salt? Well, she is ingenious, so she added the salt right then! She salted the bread! She didn't let her "mistake" stop her.

I stayed over another day or two, so the lady decided to make me some more bread. I went into the kitchen and asked, "Do you have the salt in it?" She said, "Yes!" I said, "What else do you put in bread?" She said she was putting the last ingredient in, and then it would be ready. Well, the bread turned out perfectly. As we sat down to eat, she said, "I hope to God it tastes good because I almost forgot to put in the yeast. I forgot until you came into the kitchen. I put it in last, and I've never done it that way before, so it might not be any good." This time she was taking the perspective of having "made a mistake." She was not being charitable to herself. From my perspective, the bread was perfect. I finally said, "Would you just be quiet and let me decide whether or not the bread is good. If it's not, I'll let you know. And if necessary we'll get some yeast and sprinkle on it!"

Charity truly begins at home. I see charity as that process of taking care of yourself so you are not a burden on your family, and of the family taking care of itself so it is not a burden on society. Charity is doing your work so well that people around you don't have to come along behind you and redo what you have done. Charity is handling your level of agreement and responsibility so well that people say, "I'm glad you were here. I'm glad you participated in my life."

Two actions are part of charity: an inner action and an outer action. The inner action is one of balance and the flow of love within. It is awfully hard to give when you are in a state of remorse, resentment or anger. The only way you can truly give is when you are in a state of joy, creativity and inner abundance. That state only comes about when you are exercising your spiritual gifts, your gifts of loving. When you breathe that divine love in, you feel the currents of God within your own beingness, and you feel the joy and bliss of Soul. In that moment, you could probably be fleeced by the most simple-minded con man in the whole world — and love it. When you are centered in divine love, there is no way you can be stripped of your joy. And when you have joy, you can give joy. That's the outward action of charity. When you can give joy, you can, again, receive joy. It's a marvelous cycle.

Charity is the process of both giving and receiving. What value is it to give a gift if it can't be received? Others' taking is their extending the charity back to you. This consciousness of charity has never been one-way. It takes both the giver and the receiver to complete the action. When you give back to the giver (by taking the gift), it makes you both feel good.

Some people have a hard time receiving. It often takes a great deal of smoothness and tact to receive gifts from people without embarrassing them or putting them on the spot. Years ago when people gave me things, I would say, "No, thank you." I thought I was being "spiritual" by refusing to take anything from them and just giving my joy and my love. But when I tried to give them love, there was no place for them to receive it because they felt rejected. They were experiencing a form of resentment because I hadn't let them give to me. They felt almost like they weren't worthy enough to give to me. That had never been part of my consciousness, but that was the way it was perceived. By refusing their gifts, I shut off the flow, and they could not receive what I had to give. Now I accept every present. I receive with an open heart. The flow is there, and not only is it easy for me to give love back to them, but it's also easy for them to receive my love because they feel good about the whole action. It's balanced. Then it becomes a deeper experience than just giving and receiving. It becomes a **sharing**, a form of intimacy, which is an expression of loving oneness.

When you give of your ability, your joy, your spiritual gifts and your creativity, people coming behind you (whom you may not even know) are able to partake of the spiritual blessings that you extend. We talk of Spirit and spiritual laws of acceptance, cooperation, understanding, and enthusiasm. But what value are all of these if there is no charity? Charity is the keynote that allows us to function here. You know that you must first accept yourself before you can accept others. And you must first cooperate with yourself before you can cooperate with others. So also, must you first give charity to yourself before you can give charity to others.

See the creative energy inside you. That's the Spirit of God inside. That's the primordial thrust of spiritual energy. Its form is unto itself. It is that essence of Spirit, of God, of the love that is within; it is that which activates all other forms. You look past many, many illusions in the lower worlds. You look past the illusions of the physical forms, the emotions, the mind, and the subconscious levels. You have charity toward all those levels, yet are able to look past them. You don't say to someone, "I just can't stand seeing you — get out of my way." You realize that on the path they are traveling, they may value your understanding and need your love.

Sometimes it seems easy to give love in a general sense, for example, to a large group. It can be more difficult to share love in a one-to-one relationship with your spouse, your boss or your children. Then come the trials and tribulations of, "Do I give love, or do I give animosity and resentment? Am I too tired to put energy into this relationship any longer? Why don't they love me better?" Love is of little value if you don't have charity. You give. You give. You give. And then you give more. Generally it is not man's nature to give, but it is the **hu-man's**, the God-man's, nature to give. It is the nature of the spiritual man to give.

In the process of charity, let your own love be your guide. Let the guiding Light of your own heart show you the way. Your mind won't be able to do it. Your emotions won't be able to do it. Your body won't be able to do it. You won't find charity as the essence of the mind, the emotions, or the body. Charity is of the Spirit. You can give of the Spirit through many forms. You can rub a back, give a massage, wash the dishes, or take a day off work to spend with the children. Whatever you give, give freely, expecting nothing in return. Give one-hundred percent so if someone else doesn't give back, you have given enough for both of you. Then it is complete. That's what makes it work.

This concept of charity does not conflict with your responsibility to take care of yourself. If you don't take care of yourself, you soon do not have any reserves from which to give. Many years ago I heard a lady say, "Oh, if I could just take on the aches and pains of my family, I would gladly do it." I asked, "Why?" She said, "Because I love them so much." I asked, "What are you going to do with all their aches and pains? They, by themselves, can handle what they have; but if you take on the pain of all seven of them, who's going to be in the hospital? Who is going to take care of the kids while your husband is at work? And who is he going to be worrying about all the time he's trying to work?'' She realized that she could express the greatest love for her family by allowing them to experience the things they had to experience and by keeping herself balanced and loving. That way, she could assist them when it was necessary.

You take care of yourself, and it may be necessary to let others experience their pain and tension so that they can understand what these things are and be prepared for greater things that may be coming later. They have to learn how to handle difficulties and discover their own solutions to their difficulties. Everyone grows by this process. To take things from people is to deny them their own God-consciousness. Don't worry. They'll find the solutions. They'll discover their own paths. If you point the way to the Light, they'll find their own ways. There is an old saying, ''Give a man a fish, feed him for a day; teach a man to fish, feed him for a lifetime.'' If you teach people to fish, they will feed themselves. They're free, and you're free. In freedom, the loving can be perfect. Discover where you can assist, rather than interfere. Assistance is a very beautiful form of loving.

There is something transcendental in the process of giving love. It is your very beingness that speaks when you are loving. Charity reflects the loving that is the very essence behind all creation. There is nowhere that it is not. Its very form is that of giving, and it doesn't ask anything in return. God has never approached you and said, ''Give me that.'' But God laid out examples and guidelines that we call disciplines — the disciplines that bring you into greater strength and set you free.

Charity is multidimensional. The outer form of charity is very simple. It is just expressing your joy outwardly. That outward expression may come from the mind as good thoughts, from the emotions as happiness, or from the physical as financial support or good health. To express it outwardly, you may have to exercise your creativity. It takes great sensitivity and great gentleness to give into the hearts of others without abusing them or making them feel less than the form of spiritual love they are.

Many times people are caught short in a lot of areas of living. They may say, "If I just had another gallon of gas," or "If I just had a million dollars." Well, charity is different for different people. People's needs are different, and their expressions are different. When someone shares with you or gives to you just what you need in that moment, you feel love and thankfulness flow through you. And you often want to do something in return. If it's not possible to return a blessing to the one who gave it, give it to someone else. Another form of charity may be the process of sharing with someone what has been given to you.

Charity may involve giving to a stranger, just because the person asks. If someone comes up to you and asks for bus fare home, you can help — not by asking how much it is, but by giving more than enough money and just saying, "God bless you." You'll both feel good. When you allow the love to flow freely and express through you in charity toward yourself and all others, you come closer and closer to that pure essence of the Spirit within you. As you prepare the planet for your children, for their children, and even for those who will be here three or four hundred years from now, you are exercising an even greater form of charity.

Charity can never be anything other than giving because there is only God, and God gives only to Itself. When you enter into the consciousness of the Mystical Traveler, you begin to see that essence in everything and everyone you meet. Though it manifests differently for everyone, you perceive the oneness that sustains the many differences. That oneness is charity, is loving, is the essence of God. It is your own true beingness. And the day

75

you awaken to that realization of Self will be one of the most joyful days you may ever experience.

It all comes back to the questions, "Who are you inside yourself and who are you relating to inside the other person?" If you are relating to the same energy force that is within you, the one called God, you'll find it so easy to share and extend love — not the personal love or the jealous love that says, "Do it my way or else," but the spiritual love that says, "I love you, no matter what."

Loving With Discernment

We often hold in reserve those things we value most. We may do this with the quality we incorrectly identify as love. We say, "You love me, and then I'll love you." The other person says, "You love **me**, and then I'll love you." It's a stand-off. Then you say, "Well, I'll love you a little bit and see how my love is returned." When you do this, whether the love is returned or not, you find yourself feeling short on receiving. You think you're long on the giving, but you're just as short on the giving as you are on the receiving. Then you feel there just isn't any justice. In reality, you can only receive what you are capable of giving.

It is important, at this point, to see that you must go on, regardless of your attitude. You have at least two choices of attitude. You can go on crying, or you can go on laughing. If you have the choice (and you do), you might just as well go on laughing. It's more joyful. Spirit is joyful. The nature of the Soul is joyful. The personality isn't always joyful, but it is part of the illusions of the physical level.

You test people; you test them all the time. Husbands test wives; wives test husbands. Children test parents and each other. It's often a question of, "Do you love me or not?" Often this is the end result, although it may take a different form, such as the following conversation:
"I love you."
"Then why did you do that terrible thing?"
"Because I don't love you **your** way. I love you **my** way."
"Well, your way isn't too good."

"I'll love you your way if you show me what it is."
"I'm not too sure I know....."

The fact is, we're often not sure if we want to give love. So sometimes we give love a little bit at a time. It's called "courting." We court people in many ways. Sometimes we court them for love, sometimes for a job, sometimes for opportunity. But once the goal is accomplished, we tend to forget about the process of courting, and that's a big mistake. For instance, after being married, some couples forget about courting each other. But it's the process of courting that got you your goal -- your spouse, the promotion, that job -- and it is the process of courting that will maintain it. It is that courting process of awareness, of caring and of giving which will assist you in bringing about greater spiritual success.

Love can be expressed many ways. A husband comes home and asks his wife, "Do you love me?" The wife says, "I fixed your dinner." Then a little later she asks, "Do you love me?" He says, "I gave you the paycheck." These are all forms of loving. Do you remember the movie, "Fiddler On The Roof"? Tevya asks his wife, "Do you love me?" She answers something like, "I guess so. After twenty years, I probably do. There's no one else around, so it must be you." That is one expression of love, but it's not the only way to truly build a consciousness of loving and Light. It's important to be able to tell your loved ones that you do love them, and it's important to demonstrate that loving through action.

When we speak of love scientifically, we speak of a relative position between objects held together by their interaction. But when we look more closely at this process, we discover both an attraction and a repulsion inherent in the process. The thing that attracts we often call love. The thing that repels we often call hate. In hate we reside outside of our consciousness of oneness with all things. If we reside too far out, we become inflictive in our nature.

78

Sometimes we see a person promoting the infliction on others called "tyranny of weakness." For example, a husband might say, "I'm sick, and I think I'm going to die." It scares his wife, and she says, "Oh, don't die! Don't die!" Then he thinks, "I've got her now." The next time he says, "Honey, I'm really sick. I think I'm dying," she says, "Don't die. What can I do?" He says, "Would you help me polish my shoes? I can't bend over; it hurts too much. And fix me something special for dinner." Weakness can be tyrannical.

Children are often encouraged from an early age to become tyrants through weakness. If there is a test coming up at school, the child may say, "I'm sick, Mom. Can I stay home from school?" She says, "Okay." Then right after the test is over, the child says, "I feel a lot better now. Can I watch television?" And Mom says, "Well, okay." She goes along with the action because her love is an emotional love, not the divine love of doing whatever is best for the child. She doesn't want to hurt the child, and she wants to be right. So she holds back and lets the child get away with these things, even though it might not be the best action for the child. However, if that was the worst thing that happened to us as children, God certainly loves us very much.

Can love be disturbing? No. Can the **expression** of love be disturbing? Yes. For example, if someone gets into "keeping score," it can be very disturbing. "I've given more than you have. I've measured it — thirty-four love units against your twenty-two. You owe me twelve more before I do anything else for you." This is certainly conditional loving. Do you know what **unconditional** loving is? Just walk by a new baby and take a look. That baby will reach out with its love and say, "Pick me up." And you love it so much that you want to grab it and run....until you think of all the dirty diapers. Then you would run to give it back to its mother. There is always a reality working, and that's also spiritual — practical spirituality. Any other kind

79

of spirituality is seldom workable.

Often two people meet, fall in love and marry because each one thinks the other is fantastic. Then, almost immediately, either one or both of them set about to change the other partner into someone who more closely matches their ideal. It's not too long before one says, "Let's split. You're boring. I don't love you anymore. You're not the one I married." And the other one says, "No, I'm not. You've been working to change me ever since the day we got married. If I open my mouth, you tell me to shut up. You don't want me doing the things I used to love doing. You don't want me hanging around with my old friends. I don't know what you want." It's very important to let people breathe their own air, digest their own food and express in the way that is natural for them. If you attempt to change someone's expression, you will probably meet with frustration and heartache.

Sexual expression is a form of loving and very great creativity. In a sexual relationship there is great potential to use that sexual expression to enhance and lift into your greater expression. Because this area is so powerful, there is also tremendous potential for negativity if it is not used in an uplifting way.

The creativity of the sexual center and the creativity of a spiritual center are located in a similar area of the body. This area encircles the body like a band between an area starting just below the navel and extending to an area of the thighs about five to six inches below the buttocks. Both sexual creativity and a spiritual creativity are located in that area. When people feel a surging of Spirit, they often translate it as a sexual urge. So they release that urge in a sexual encounter and find it doesn't always bring satisfaction. Particularly, it does not bring satisfaction when it is not accompanied by spiritual loving, caring and sharing with a partner that is part of a total, loving relationship.

Many times, not knowing that the level of sexual expression and creative expression are located very close together within the physical body, you become confused in your feeling. A level inside of you **seems** to urge for sexual expression when it may, in reality, be urging toward creative expression. It may seem to be saying, "Let's go have sexual intercourse," because that is the experience to which you've conditioned yourself. But it may really be saying, "Create — bring forth something new out of your own beingness." If this is so, the sense of satisfaction from sexual intercourse will be short-lived. Your satisfaction and fulfillment will last much longer if you lift yourself in a creative expression of Spirit.

There are a lot of different ways to express sexuality. None are necessarily good or bad. There is no morality in Spirit that determines a "right" or "wrong" way. Morality is an aspect of society. Man makes his own morality, and man's morality determines who is a "sexual deviant." Personally, I don't use the words "pervert" or "deviate" because that brings in attitudes of right and wrong, and there are no intrinsic rights or wrongs. There are, however, wide variations of sexual expression so I prefer the term "sexual variant." There are ways that bring joy and ways that do not. There are ways that bring loving contentment, and there are ways that bring loneliness and despair. It's everyone's choice to express however they feel comfortable. People usually discover for themselves the ways that bring fulfillment and joy.

When you get high enough above the negative levels of body consciousness, you can experience spiritual liberation. Then you can enjoy the lower levels with less chance of getting caught in the illusions of those levels. That does not, however, give you any sort of license to abuse or misuse those levels. It's important to be judicious about your activities, selective in your experiences and wise in your approach.

Different sexual expressions produce different results, and some are much easier to handle than others. One result of a great deal of unselective sexual expression can be a disease in the body, such as venereal disease. Another result can be the scattering of a lot of creative energy which could be channeled into other areas of positive direction and fulfillment. Another result might be confusion and a loss of identity because of mixing too many different frequencies into the body. When you are not aware of some of these results, you may not notice that they are happening. People who have had many sexual experiences from a young age may not have other reference points, so they may not notice. However, the body seems to suffer from energy debilitation and strange forms of dis-ease.

As you become more spiritually aware, you discover a more solid sense of your own energy. As you do spiritual exercises and become involved in meditation and contemplation, you begin to discover your own identity. Then if you go out and involve yourself in a casual sexual encounter, the sense of mixed energies and confusion may become very noticeable and may become a choice you avoid.

Sexual intercourse is a very rapid way to mix the frequencies of your own beingness with those of your partner. So when sexual intercourse is done indiscriminately, it **can be** a rapid way to lose your own identity. In becoming confused about who you really are, you may lose your conscious direction. You can also lose your positive thrust of energy and feel extremely depleted and drained. If you have a sexual relationship with someone who is having many sexual encounters with others, you can not only receive the frequencies of your partner, but you can also receive the frequencies of those with whom your partner has had sexual relations. You may become the "garbage collector," and that can be hell. The result may be that you become so unsure of your own identity and self-worth that you give up the dignity of your consciousness and allow the lower desire patterns of your nature to run your life.

Promiscuous sexual encounters can confuse you on many levels. Because the sexual creativity and the spiritual creativity are located so closely together, sexual activity can adversely affect your spiritual creativity, leaving you even more open to pick up the energy of the last person you encountered in sexual relations. When you enter into this type of confusion, you find it affecting many areas of your life.

If you are going to have a sexual relationship, do yourself a favor and have it with the most enlightened person you can find — and have an exclusive relationship with that one person. If your partner is not interested in an exclusive sexual relationship, the choice of how to handle it is always up to you. Just be aware that you may be leaving yourself open to great discord and confusion. There are no rights or wrongs; there are, however, different results from different actions.

God dwells in essence within each person. Keep that in mind in a sexual relationship and love that other person as you would love the God that dwells within them. Expressing sexually is one way the Soul makes love on the physical level. When you are loving your partner from the physical, emotional, mental and spiritual levels simultaneously, there can be a very beautiful exchange of all energies. You can experience a balancing and a blending that is truly satisfying and fulfilling, not only on the sexual level, but on all other levels of your beingness.

When two people are loving each other, they don't necessarily look to each other for fulfillment. Rather, they find themselves looking in the same **direction** for their fulfillment. That's the key. Look to the Spirit for your fulfillment. Look to your Self for your fulfillment. When two people do this, they turn to look at each other and see the fullness they both express, and the loving of each other enhances and amplifies their fullness. Then they can't seem to do anything wrong. Everything they do becomes spiritually right and perfect. And the sexual love is then one aspect of the total loving relationship.

Loving From Strength

P eople often place much of their sense of identity with the body. It's illusionary. You are so much more than your body. A man once told me, "My wife says she can't live without me, but I can't talk to her about the things that really mean a lot to me. She doesn't care to listen and share on that level. Apparently she just wants my body. So I fill it up with alcohol and give it to her." That's the way he solved the problem of her needs for his body. But he was not happy with that solution and neither was she. It wasn't sharing. It wasn't loving. I talked with them and explained about the various levels of consciousness and how, in loving, that loving can be expressed on every level. They saw how their loving was fragmented and incomplete. They worked at bringing it into expression on every level, and their marriage became better and better.

The Light of your own consciousness will show you where you are not completing the truth of your Self within yourself. The truth within you is complete, though it is often veiled by illusion so that you do not know or perceive it clearly. The great quest of human nature is to seek the Truth that will encompass everything, the Truth within which everything will fall and within which everything can be accounted for, measured and handled. The belief is that when this is accomplished, peace, happiness and security will be found because there will be a place for everything. The quest itself is an illusion. The only way the quest can be accomplished is to know God. God is the only Truth that encompasses everything else.

In the physical sense, God is rather intangible, and our

conditioning teaches us to go after **tangible** things — more money, a better job, a big house, a new car, a husband, a wife, a good physique, a cute figure, new clothes, and so forth. As you pursue these goals, many things can happen. You may use other people to get the things you want, and others may use you to get what they want. But on this level, everybody uses everybody. That's really okay. It's part of the game here. **Abuse** and **misuse** are not part of the game. But **use** — sure. You use people; people use you. It's an exchange. Nobody can exploit or abuse you unless you allow it, promote it, or actively create it. You can do all three. But without your permission on some level, you cannot be abused.

We all get what we ask for. Sometimes we ask for things consciously, knowing what we are doing; sometimes we ask for things in a not-so-conscious way, but we still ask for them. Women who wear low-cut blouses or very short skirts or very tight pants are asking for the attention they get. They ask for possible exploitation and when men do exploit them, they feel misused and abused. That may be so, but they created it in a very specific way.

What about the man who buys lavish gifts for his women? Very often he is attempting to buy love, affection and the esteem of those for whom he is buying the gifts. And when they take the gifts and leave him, he feels misused and taken advantage of. Perhaps it is so, and if it is, he set himself up for it.

Be wise in your approach. Observe your own behavior, and use your intelligence to tell you what the result will be. It's really not too difficult. If the result is okay with you, the action is okay. And if you don't like the result your behavior brings you, direct your behavior in a way that brings you more comfortable results. These things are not big mysteries when you look at them clearly.

A lady who was divorced from her husband came to me

for counseling. She was still experiencing some difficulty regarding her divorce, and she related to me how the divorce had come about. She and her husband were making love, and the television happened to be on and tuned to "The $64,000 Question." They were extremely involved in their love-making, and he was particularly involved with the action. About that time the $32,000 question was asked, and like a shot out of the blue, she answered it. Well, everything was over — instantly. He got up, showered, dressed, packed a bag, said, "Would you like to try for $64,000?" and walked out the door. That was the last she saw of him; his attorney handled all the divorce proceedings. She told me, "Sometimes you have to be very careful the questions you answer!" Timing **is** important. Sometimes it's wise to defer things until the timing is more appropriate.

If the love you express is not the love of spiritual unfoldment, you find yourself caught in areas of lack and emotional pain. If you are going into a relationship with someone, let him or her know how far you can go at the moment, and if you don't know, just say, "I don't know." There is great security in that statement because the honesty is evident. Maybe you don't know because of the way your partner asked, or maybe there are other reasons. But there is a security in knowing you are not going to give dishonest information and let your loved one flounder in confusion. There is nothing wrong with just saying, "I don't know."

If you work with people by loving and assisting them without interfering, you are becoming a Light worker in action. Then you start attuning to the Light within each person, the quality that is called the Christ. Each person has a Light within them. Your job is simply to become aware of it. When you do, you can activate it into a greater and greater consciousness, until you reach into the Soul that is the consciousness of God and Light and Love. The Soul is well-protected. It is guarded by the best guardians you will ever find. Some of those guardians are, "Woe is me," "Nobody loves me," "I am all messed up," "I am ruined," "I am going to hell," "'I hate your guts," "I am green-eyed with jealousy," "I want you" and "I want to control you." A key to bypassing all this is just to say, "Okay," and go on with your life. None of these states lasts for very long. The consciousness that is the Soul outlasts them all. Don't fight or resist negativity because that resistance will lock you to the negative. Just let it be what it is and flow through you and right on out of you. Let it go. And direct your action in a positive way by **using everything** that comes your way as a stepping-stone to where you're going.

It's often important to turn off the distractions of the physical world and turn toward the essence of Spirit. You may want to go away by yourself or go up to the mountains, which can symbolize your higher consciousness. There you may be able to see yourself and God more clearly. When you are down in the valley, there are more shadows. Similarly, in every consciousness there are peaks and valleys. Often you climb to a peak in your consciousness and feel so good, but then you start coasting down the other side into the valley of shadows. Instead of coasting into those things, it might be wise to sit on the pinnacle of the mountain for awhile and enjoy the height which you've reached. It's much easier to work from a position of knowledge and strength than a position of weakness and inadequacy.

Feelings of discouragement and despair come in when you are not realizing who you really are. You don't feel God within. You don't feel the Soul, the Spirit or the bliss of your inner consciousness. So you may do anything in order to feel **something.** You might even perpetrate pain upon yourself in order to feel something. You might strike out at other people so they will strike back so that you will feel. You might gorge yourself with food or drink or use drugs or what-have-you — all to get some feeling so you can say,

"Maybe that's me." I **can** guarantee that's **not** you. You are **not** the food or the alcohol or the drugs; you are **not** your pain, your hurt, your confusion. You are **not** your feelings. What you are trying to define in terms of these levels does not reside there. If it did, you would have found it a long time ago. The joy, bliss and love that well up inside of you like a great fountain are from God, the God that resides both within you and outside of you.

You can ask for the Light of the Christ to activate your own Christ consciousness. If you have been putting yourself in a position to receive, you may experience a flash of knowing, of awareness, of realization. When you are working in psychic areas, realizations can often be fearful because they come too fast, with too little preparation. When you work under the protection of the Mystical Traveler consciousness, you will be prepared for your awakening. The Traveler will bring the realizations to your consciousness more gradually. The veil that covers you from yourself will be pulled back slowly, and you will reveal yourself to yourself in a gradual progression. You will come to know that you are one with the Father, who is one with all His creation. Then you can look at all things and express your oneness with the simple statement, "This I am."

Even after confronting
your karma, your
negative habits will
attempt to pull you
back into the old,
familiar patterns.

Karma Is Spelled S.T.U.P.I.D.

Chapter Four

In its purest sense, karma can be defined as "action." And **negative** karma can be defined as **inability** to act. Often it is your negative karma that is upon you when you don't know which way to turn or where to go. You say, "Which way do I go? Do I go here or do I go there? Do I choose this or do I choose that? I don't know what to do!" That's your karma. You feel like you should move one way, but something inside says, "Don't" or "I can't." And you don't know what to do or which direction to take. You can't even "cop out" and make a decision by default; your karma has completely bound you. You're caught. Sometimes you don't even know it, and that's when ignorance may seem like a blessing.

When you have karma and don't know it, you go trudging right along, encountering one karmic thing after another, until you feel like a big wheel going in circles. That feeling may be accurate. Sometimes you keep circling over and over the same karmic situation until one day you wake up and say, "Haven't I done this before? I remember the last time. I didn't like it much then, and now it seems like it's happening again." **Pay attention** this time. **Focus** on what is happening. **Discipline** yourself in the action. If you can focus and become aware, you can act: "I don't have to do that anymore. I'll do this instead." And in that moment of positive **action**, your negative karma has been confronted and dissolved by your intelligence — by seeing

91

what it is and making a choice.

Even after confronting your karma, your negative habits will attempt to pull you back into the old familiar patterns. Allowing that to happen is spelled S.T.U.P.I.D. Those negative habits may be so strong within you that when the intellect says, "Watch it!", they say, "But I got through this before. It's okay." Some of these karmic patterns are like arsenic. You can drink a little bit, and it won't kill you, and you can drink a little bit more, and it won't kill you. But one day you drink a little more and you're **dead**. It accumulates in the system, and you can't get rid of it. You don't even have to drink it on consecutive days. You can space it out over a long period of time, and it still accumulates and eventually kills you.

Ignorance and the inability to act kills. But it tortures first. Stupidity tortures, too. You get into the same "mess" over and over. Maybe it's the same scene with your parents. Maybe it's the same affair with different women. Maybe it's the same surrender to alcohol. Whatever form it takes, it is the inability to change that traps you in a pattern. And you say, "I just keep doing it to myself. I don't know why. I can't seem to get out of it. It hurts." You're hitting yourself in the head; of course, it hurts. Stop that, and maybe your headache will clear up. And if you have an inability to stop, find somebody who can help you stop. Have somebody sit on your hand. Or bind it. Sure, that's a ridiculous point of view, but sometimes it takes drastic change to force you into a new direction, a positive action.

People addicted to gambling are an example of negative patterns in action. A gambler keeps putting his money out and keeps losing. The guy is sitting there gambling, and it's like some other guy comes along with a baseball bat and hits him on the side of the head. The gambler says, "Wow! Some guy hit me on the side of the head with a baseball bat." And he goes on gambling.

Pretty soon, the guy with the bat comes back, and the gambler says, "Look at that guy with the baseball bat; he's going to hit me on the side of the head again." He does, and the gambler says, "Did you see what he did? He hit me on the side of the head with a baseball bat." And he goes back to gambling. The guy comes and hits him again, and the gambler says, "Can you believe that? He hit me **again**." And he goes back to gambling. The next time the guy comes around and hits him on the side of the head, he says, "I think I'll get out of here!" And he leaves.

Seeing it coming isn't enough. Sure you're a good prophet; your prophecies are accurate. Here it comes! Whack! Right in the head! Knowing it's coming doesn't make it any nicer. And it doesn't make the hurt any less. After the first hit, you could be getting up and vacating the chair, getting prepared to duck or doing some negotiating. When a karmic field comes your way, get up and move. Often that karmic field comes to you to **get** you to move, to **get** you up off that chair and moving into new things that will be to your advantage. Change is a necessary part of life. Resisting change more often than not brings pain.

Some people are terrific at resisting change. They say, "Not me. I've been sitting in this spot for twenty years, and I'm not moving for any old karmic thing that hits me in the head." **All right, get hit in the head.** "No, I don't want to get hit in the head." **Then move!** "I ain't movin'." **Here it comes!** "Darn, right in the head. That hurt! But I won't let it get to me. I ain't movin'." **Why?** " 'Cuz I'm proud!" **Your head is starting to look like a sack of doorknobs. You'd better get rid of that pride in a hurry!** "No, sir, I'm going to sit here in this spot until kingdom come." **Here it comes again!** "Ouch! Right in the head!"

How often do you have to get hit in the head and knocked down before you say, "This isn't working!"? Sometimes, before you reach this point, you start getting numb. You get hit in the head and think, "That didn't hurt

93

so much." Perhaps your scalp is black and blue and crusted over and numb. Maybe you get so used to it you think it's getting better. **Here it comes again!** "That didn't hurt too bad." Maybe not, but this time your jaw was knocked out of place. It's starting to affect all sorts of things.

The repercussions of a karmic action do go through the body and the consciousness and affect many areas. For instance, the pattern of stubbornness and resistance in a woman can cause disease in the reproductive system and necessitate a hysterectomy. Those karmic baseball bats come around. You get hit. If you resist pain by continually clamping down and pushing negative energy down into the reproductive area of the body, that energy blocks the flow and can eventually manifest as dis-ease. It's a blockage of energy. This pattern in men may cause impotency or a hernia. True, the immediate cause of a hernia may be lifting something too heavy, but a pattern of resistance and stubbornness created the weakness that made the injury possible.

If you're really honest with yourself and living in truth, you can write on a piece of paper everything that has happened to you and how you caused it. It really is interesting to find out you not only created it, but allowed it, and sometimes even promoted it. Then you want to blame somebody else for your creation — "Oh, no. Here it comes again. He hit me on the head again! When is that going to stop?" **Get out of the way. Sitting there promotes it.** "No, it doesn't. I'm just sitting here minding my own business." **Okay, but the guy with the bat runs on a track, and he runs through here every two hours. Why are you sitting on the track?** "I didn't know it was a track because it was dark when I sat down." **It's light now and in a few minutes, he's coming around again. Get up! Move!** "No, sir, I'm not moving." **They're building another track. There are going to be two guys with bats, one on each side.** "I don't think I can take that. I'll move. But it isn't my fault. I shouldn't have to move." **Yes, you do have to move.**

94

The first time you get hit with that bat, the first time you see it coming, the first time you hear its approach — that's the time to move. Don't wait for it to hit you fifteen times. Don't hang onto the old patterns. Let them go. Drop them and move on to what's next. It's called intelligence.

I hear many people talk about their suffering, but when I look across the planet, I see the Light — perfect in its balance and its manifestation. I see people working through, balancing and clearing their karmic situations. I see people growing, progressing, learning, coming into greater and greater positions of awareness. And that's not suffering. Suffering occurs when man alienates himself from God. All else that is called suffering is only a symptom of this separation from God.

When you do not see the perfection of the Light action and your path upon this planet, the action of the Light sometimes appears to be happenstance, and that can cause a form of suffering. For instance, one week you may call in the Light and find it really works for you and that everything in your life happens in a beautiful way. A week later you may call in the Light and find that **nothing** seems to happen the way it should. You say, "It didn't work." You feel the suffering. Did you ever consider that the rough time you seem to be having might be just what you need to help you grow, to help you lift into the next level of awareness? The Light always works for your highest good, though it may not always be apparent to you what your highest good is.

At times in your life you may feel like you've mixed several things together and suddenly transmuted a "lead" into a "gold" so precious and beautiful that it's beyond words. Then you forget what things you mixed together in what proportions, and you can't do it again. That can produce the form of suffering that comes with the inability to re-create the beauty that once happened. Yet that beauty was for then, and the human consciousness always moves forward into an eternal NOW. So it's important to live in the moment and create anew in each moment the "gold" of your beingness. You can never do it by using yesterday's formula. It is made new all the time.

My job often consists of alleviating pain within myself and others. Within myself it's very easy. I just move into the high consciousness and reside there until I see things in a greater perspective. I may be experiencing many things on this level which may not be seen as being positive or loving, but if I recognize God is everywhere and see evidence of God in total existence, my "suffering" also comes into perspective, and I see and understand the perfection of the greater action.

When you feel yourself to be in a position of suffering, you can almost bet that you have created that suffering for yourself. You may find yourself saying, "I need help, I need advice; these things happened and I have to find a way to solve this." What you are really saying is, "I did this and this and this, and now it's all come back to me, and it hurts." When this happens, you have two choices: you can laugh or you can cry — but you have to handle it. You can stay in the feeling of misery and despair and cry over what has happened. Or you can start lifting yourself and say, "Well, it sure hurts when I laugh, but I'll laugh anyway." You'll feel so much better with the second choice. It might not take away the suffering, but it could make it easier to go through.

One attitude you can take when you have caused yourself pain and discomfort through your actions is one of quietness and serenity. That attitude can sustain you through almost anything. Focus on the moment without looking ahead to next week or next month or next year. Just hold yourself present in the now — at each point — and deal with whatever presents itself to you in the moment. Usually life is not too difficult that way. Much suffering seems to occur when you look back into yesterday or forward into tomorrow.

When God created the world, he looked out at His creation and said, "It's good." Yet there are so many religions that say man was born to suffering and that man must suffer for his sins. So whatever this thing called sin is must be inside, not out in the world. It has been said that sin is ignorance, and it's true that a lot of suffering comes about because we don't know what's going on. Ignorance is darkness, and in the darkness, you sometimes fall. It could be said that in this way, you sin against your own Christ consciousness, the Light of your own Self.

Living Successfully

One concept that mankind has developed from darkness, ignorance and lack of understanding is that of **punishment**. The practice of punishment has caused much suffering in the world. The idea of punishment seems to be a universal one, with many different aspects. One type of punishment is a person's reaction to someone different from themselves — "I punish you because you are not like me and because you are not doing things the way I want you to do them." If this idea is presented to those doing the punishing, they may say, "No, that isn't why I'm punishing you." So you might say, "Then you must feel like you have a right to punish me. What is your right to punish me?" If they say, "Because I'm your parent," you may have to say, "Okay." But children often add, "Then when I am older and out on my own and am no longer under your control, I can punish **you**." That brings forth another aspect of punishment, which is **getting even**. This is the old law of Moses: "An eye for an eye and a tooth for a tooth." On the lower levels, this is often an accurate point of view. But the Bible also says that vengeance will be the Lord's. The supreme God dispenses absolute balance, and that is not punishment. **Man** punishes. God **loves**. God loves equally men who punish and men who receive punishment.

You may enter into dispensing punishment when you feel you're being hemmed in, when you find somebody crowding in on you, when someone is usurping your authority over your own domain — "What right have you to look in my books?" "What right do you have to ask how much money I have?" When you have established your sovereign divinity over the things you say are **yours**, you really feel right and justified in punishing whoever gets into that area. But when you reach out to punish someone else, you're actually punishing yourself; you're really saying, "I just can't handle it any other way."

I'd like to relate a personal experience as an example of how punishment is self-defeating. I have two dogs at home who may be smarter than anyone else in the house. When they were still pretty young, we were fixing a barrier so they could have one part of the house and leave us the rest of the house — as sort of a compromise. But the dogs wanted the part of the house where I was. Many hours were spent devising a way to keep them hemmed into a small area of the house. We'd get the barrier ready, put them on the other side, and call them with a whistle — to see if they'd find a way to overcome whatever obstacle we'd placed in front of them. We tried a lot of ways — without much success. Finally, those who were working on this thought they had really come up with a "foolproof" barrier. So we put them on the other side, sat back, and watched them get through. One dog got through a space only a couple of inches wide, a space that objectively he could never have gotten through. I was watching the auras of the others in the room, and some reflected the impulse to grab the dog and "cram" him right back through the hole — with love, naturally. And some of the auras reflected the impulse to hit him with something so he wouldn't try that again. I saw these things, so I thought I'd demonstrate this type of action to them. I picked up a piece of paper and hit it hard on the floor in front of the dog, and the dog backed off from that opening. But he found his way through another before too long. He wasn't going to let anything stop him. Both dogs are smart. They learned to get through that "restriction," and we constructed another one, which they also learned to get through. It took us quite awhile before we found a way to keep them within a certain area. We could have punished them, and they would have stopped getting through the barrier. We could have hit them so hard they would have become very fearful. But we would

99

have lost them as soon as we'd done that. Punishment is a losing proposition. Sometimes people do learn in punishment, yet they will learn much more effectively through positive reinforcement and loving.

Most people have been punished a great deal in their lives, and sometimes the punishment is in not being allowed to think for themselves. People don't allow children to think; they think for them — "Do as you're told and don't talk back. And don't you dare question me." A child loves to ask, "Why?" You explain something, and they say, "Why?" You explain more, and they say, "Why?" You love them, so you explain more, and they say, "Why?" So you explain more, and you think they've got it, and they say, "Why?" And about that time you punish them by either smacking them or giving them some nonsense statement they know is not true. And right there you create a breakdown in communication that may affect the next forty years — and you'll know you did it by punishing the child who asked, "Why?"

Maybe the child doesn't want to know **why**. Possibly he wants to know **how does it work?** When a child asks, "Why?" he may be asking how something works or how he can work it. So that's what you answer to. One time I was with friends and their child was asking about washing with soap, and his parents were explaining to him how soap washes the dishes and the clothes. He kept asking "why" questions until they said a few words which I'm sure they didn't really mean. When they were through, I picked the child up, put him on the sink, turned on the water, put soap in his hands and started rubbing them together so we got lots of suds and bubbles. I said, "Now do you understand why?" He said, "Yes." He saw what happened with soap. He didn't need to know any other information. Information wasn't his level. His level was, **"How does this thing do it?"** Words did not satisfy him because he did not understand the words after being told them. But he did understand how it worked. He did understand the experience.

If someone asks you a question and you have to punish them, it's because you have failed to show them how it works or to explain to them how to do it. People are usually after the experience of something rather than the information. If you can bring an experience to people that shows them a way to expand the range of their creativity, you are communicating successfully.

Guidelines have been presented by the Masters of all the ages, guidelines for living your life in the Light of the Christ, in the Light of your own consciousness, free of suffering. These guidelines help you handle yourself in this world. Not handling this world too well does not stop your spiritual growth, but you'll be happier if you are handling it rather well. So if you want to be happier, it is your responsibility to learn those things that make it easier to live a successful, uplifting life here.

Because it is your responsibility to handle this level, no one can really tell you what to do, and you cannot enforce blame on anyone else for what happens to you in this life. As choices present themselves to you, you sometimes enter into confusion, doubt and bewilderment. "Tomorrow" then becomes fraught with fear because you can't predict what's going to happen. That fear becomes a form of suffering. Again, you must bring yourself present in the "NOW" and live in that moment. It's easier to be happy in the moment.

Sometimes suffering comes when you have placed too much value and importance on the physical world and have become caught in the glamour of this world and all the things that exist here. You must not forget that this physical world is only ten percent of your total existence and that the ninety percent of your existence in the spiritual worlds is where much of your focus and your attention could be going.

101

When you confuse your spirituality with the materiality of this world, you're asking for big trouble. When you seek after material things and look to the world for fulfillment, you may find a temporary sense of contentment and satisfaction, but you will not find fulfillment. The trap is in mistaking the feeling of satisfaction for that of true fulfillment and thinking you've made it. At that point, the thing, person or job upon which you based your satisfaction goes, and you are left with "nothing." That's suffering.

As long as you are in the world, you must deal with the world. But it's important to keep this world and the things of this world in perspective. A great Indian Master was asked what it was like to transcend thought and reside in pure intellect. His answer was, "I don't know," which didn't make him look too good. But think about that question. From a state that transcends thought, there is no way to answer a question that comes from thought and requires thought to answer. There is no answer to that question. From a state beyond thought, there can be no description of that state in words.

It's possible to reach to a state of bliss, of oneness, of joy, that is beyond thought and beyond words. And in those moments, you see the perfection and the beauty of God's plan for each person as well as for all mankind. In those moments, you know there is no suffering and all is perfect. When you do spiritual exercises and focus upon Spirit and the sacred names of God, you reach more often into this state of knowingness and find less and less concern with the cares of the world. You transcend the barrier that causes suffering and walk free in your consciousness of God.

When you are in
a state of cooperation,
your attitude is one of
joy, enthusiasm
and abundance.

Everybody Wins

Chapter Five

As you begin to move in the direction of your own spiritual inner awareness, you may begin to work with higher vibratory rates of energy of which few people are aware. I'm going to explain a few aspects of this work to you as scientifically as I can. Spirit is the purest essence in all creation, including the worlds of the physical plane and the worlds of the higher planes. Since it is pure essence, anything that manifests must manifest from Spirit.

Scientists have traced the elements of creation back to sub-atomic particles, but they don't know what is beyond. Sub-atomic particles are manifestations from Spirit. They can be created or brought together by the power of the mind. It is because the mind has a tremendous amount of power that it is important to be very careful in the use of it.

Electrons can be built by bringing mental forces into a circular formation, a movement, a state which is not static. As we bring one electron forward, we bring it into a cohesiveness, and very soon we can form an atom. Then we bring more electrons together and form more atoms. And as we do this, we start forming energy patterns and matter.

When you reach a point of mastership of creation, you can manifest from the ethers whatever you want. There is a Master in India who can do these particular things. He is such a Master of this action that he doesn't have to sit down and gather the energy together through the method I just described. He simply commands it mentally and brings whatever he wishes to create into physical existence. He would say, it manifests itself into a physical reality. In MSIA, we use this energy to elevate ourselves and others into a higher state of consciousness by radiating this energy through the consciousness and increasing the energy level of the body.

Let's look at how this energy level works in consciousness. When our mind starts creating, it can create from the emotional point of view. In other words, we can create both positively and negatively. We can create positively by bringing our vibratory rate into a sense of perfect creation, a sense of fulfilling accomplishment and a sense of divine order, knowing that what we bring into existence will be perfect — not only that it **can** be perfect, but that it **will** be perfect. As we **become** positive, we become creators. We can start creating our balance around us.

As we see things in perfection within our minds, we can create that perfection around us. So if we see someone as imperfect, we're not helping that person into his or her perfection. But if we use someone's imperfect expression as a guideline to direct that person to lift higher, that is not negative creation; that is direction. In other words, if we point out how a negative function can lead into a positive function, that is useful as a direction. It's very important to keep the idea of the **creating** of negativity and the **directing** of negativity separate, because they are separate processes designed to bring different things into the force field around you.

Let's look at negative creation so we can see more clearly the positive creation. There is ample evidence of negative creation. If you have ever been in a home or in an area where there has been great negativity toward the Soul in a human body, you will understand what I mean.

Tremendous expression of negativity does pull in a certain force field, which will continue to create more negativity by pulling more of that force to itself.

Let me give you an example from my personal experience of this type of negative creation. While I was on the island of Nassau in the Bahama Islands, I went into the catacombs and the dungeons where people long ago had been tortured to death, had their bodies torn asunder through various methods. Walking into the catacombs, I immediately tuned into all of the negative energy that had been created there. This tremendous negative energy was so strong that I had the feeling of not being able to breathe. I filled my body with the Light and was then able to hold the negativity off.

The negativity of the catacombs was still **very** oppressive. So I thought, "What is this? Am I a victim of claustrophobia?" But I'm not prone to that experience, so I had to find out more about my feeling. I started tuning in more closely to the environment, and then I could see ghost forms starting to appear. They were probably always there, but I had to tune into them to see exactly what they were. I could feel the agony of what these people had gone through in their consciousnesses. From the agony they expressed, they had built great negative energy forms of hate, despair, agony, revenge and death around their bodies. It was extremely oppressive.

This type of death involving torture and mayhem had probably gone on there for many, many years. The victims had pledged toward hate and revenge the energy they had created through their agony and despair and emotional upset, and they had placed it in that area. The air had been so charged over all the years with this type of activity that nothing had been able to break it up, which explained the oppressive condition.

I thought that I was the "Lone Ranger" in my feelings,

that I was the only one sensing all this. But as we all walked out, I could hear people saying, "Oh, I could hardly wait to get out of that place. It was so oppressive. I could feel things on my neck and shoulders. I couldn't breathe." I started listening and realized people tune in whether they know it or not. Those people didn't know what they were sensing, but they had tuned in on the negativity, the depression and the fear. Others said, "You could just smell death in there, couldn't you?" I hadn't smelled death, but I certainly could feel it and see it.

This experience points up the fact that you can create this negativity around you through the agony, despair and fear of your own expression. You do the same thing when you are depressed and negative within your own consciousness during the day. You go out of balance within yourself, lose control and create a negative field around yourself which pulls in even more negativity. You start pulling negativity into you so fast that you wonder how on earth you can handle it, and that day can really be a bad one for you. It can be so heavily laden within your heart, stomach, neck, shoulders and eyes that you wonder how you can get through it all. You may try to knock these feelings away and find you can't. All you can do is create more and more of the negativity and pull it around you until it becomes oppressive to your body.

However, God, in His love and His great intelligence, allows us to put our bodies down and leave them at night. Then we can reach into different realms and recharge ourselves with the positive energy to bring back into the body the next morning. That's what most people do, but the people who have been in the throes of negative creation day after day after day may not get out of the body at night. The negativity suppresses them and holds them in, and they get up in the morning just as tired, just as angry, just as irritable as they were the day before. This feeling comes in the first moment they open their eyes in the morning — "Oh, another day" — and they turn on their automatic reaction patterns in the brain and start running a "movie" in their minds of what the day is going to be like.

That "movie" is often a horror show, depicting how things are going to go all wrong the entire day. Then their day starts going just like their "movie." They say, "I knew this day was going to be a bad day when I got up this morning. I knew this was going to happen when I got to work. I knew that was going to happen when I came home." They were right. They created the negative energy field, and it went ahead of them and brought into physical manifestation those things they created in their mind.

This creative force is very impersonal. It doesn't care about positive or negative. Whatever you create with it is what you get. We all see people who create negative things within their bodies so that their physical aura manifests a very negative field in it. You might look at them and say, "Oh, I don't like their aura." You might say, "I don't like the touch of them. I don't like the feelings I get when I'm around them. I feel really funny inside." And you start backing off and pulling yourself in, trying to protect yourself from coming into contact with that energy field. People do this without even knowing what they're doing.

The inadequate use of the intellect by the human race after all the centuries of negative creation is really something to behold. People still don't know that the mind has been placed within the body to help the Soul discern what is going on in the physical realm. So the mind has to be a master dynamo to fulfill that function. And it is. As creators, you have a real challenge ahead of you — to create **responsibly.** Jesus once said that you are what you think. He didn't come out and say, "You draw energy fields to yourself and charge them with negativity." He used the words that were applicable in that time and place in which he lived.

In referring to the creation of these energy fields, we

are referring to the universal creative energy of Spirit — not necessarily the pure Holy Spirit, but the creative energy of the lower realms which is positive and negative in its balance. If the negative is not balanced by the positive in these lower realms, we pull ourselves into the imbalance around us. So we are often our own worst enemies. Yet our minds are so powerful that we can, with a little bit of positiveness, create something to offset the negativity.

You know that the earth is more negative than positive. Look around the world and see it. All of the negativity being thrown up, all of the destruction, is a trap. It makes you lose track of the positive nature of the Soul, the positive nature of your own divine Self and Spirit. It's important to hold the image of your own divinity and the perfection of your own Soul. These positive aspects of yourself are the parts that are lasting and enduring.

Some years ago, there were a series of racial riots in the United States, and we could see a negative process build from a very slight incident of negativity. The emotions of the people involved added to it and started creating larger patterns of negativity. Other people started tuning into this expression, and it quickly grew into a massive group force field that just swept over people, controlled their minds and created patterns of action involving all sorts of hate and destruction. There have also been situations of extreme negativity at many of our world's universities, within national governments and between nations. Many of these actions can be observed to be the result of negative force fields which are created and allowed to function without any effective positive direction or control.

Your first line of defense in a situation of negativity is the positive use of your creative mind. You must stand as a beacon of positive energy if you are to break free of negative controls and move into a higher Light expression. You can do this both individually and as a group action.

110

Sometimes you may get up in the morning and be so positive in your mind and so dynamic in your emotions that you feel like you can accomplish anything that day. Later that night, you may go to bed feeling you have been dragged through a knothole. You say, "How can I ever get up tomorrow when I'm so dead tired tonight? And how can I feel this tired when I woke up feeling so good this morning?" It is because you are giving forth your Light. But you'll also find that you can recharge yourself rapidly.

When you are a positive power, a "lighthouse," that positiveness will go out to people. You bless every person you walk by during the day when that Light energy is flowing through you. When you walk by someone and, either out loud or silently, say, "God bless you," the power of the mind will send positive energy out to that person.

I have told young people whose parents fight a lot, "When your parents are fighting, just sit or stand nearby and say over and over in your mind, 'God bless you.'" Some of the youngsters have done this and reported back that although their parents were fighting and really upset with each other, pretty soon they just got quiet and walked away. And later they started kidding around a little bit, and everything was all right again.

There are other "magic" words besides "God bless you" that create positiveness. Silently saying "God bless you" can certainly change people, but if you really want to watch them change in a hurry, silently say, "I love you." They become absolutely elated! The negativity goes, and the positive energy sweeps in. Love is a cohesive power that brings everything together. Love has the potential to change it all into positive action and positive flow of Spirit.

Cooperating With What Is

O ne of the greatest keys that anyone could give you to create your own happiness and well-being would be the key of unconditional cooperation. That means cooperating with everything that's going on. If people express themselves in an illiterate way that you don't appreciate, keep in mind that they're not better or worse than you just because they don't talk the way you do. And if others have very flowery language and are well-educated and cultured, that doesn't mean they are better or worse than you, either. Acceptance, then, is a big part of cooperation — accepting people for who they are and seeing past the expression of the moment into the message they deliver from their hearts.

People don't like to admit they're not cooperating. I'm sure you might say, "I'm cooperating. I mean, I get up every morning and go to work. I'm there on time. I leave on time. I keep my mouth shut and stay out of trouble. I'm cooperating." That may be minimum cooperation, and that may get minimum results. But what about the better, greater things you'd like to create in your life? What about the more creative job, more money and greater happiness? How are you blocking the cooperation with your world that would bring those greater things to you?

Attitude is one key. When you are in a state of cooperation, your attitude is one of joy, enthusiasm and abundance. When you're asked to do something, you let the one who asks know that your cooperation extends far beyond what you were asked to do. **You do it more fully and more completely than they had even thought to suggest.** You may find that when you are really in a state of cooperation,

112

you not only do what is asked, you see beyond that to the next project and start preparing for that immediately. Your focus is beyond yourself and your immediate job. You are exercising your creativity and manifesting your joy. It's a joyful attitude.

In a cooperative attitude you don't look at a new assignment as, "Oh, darn, I just finished one thing and they're going to load me up with something else." Rather, your attitude is, "What can I do to assist you? Maybe I can think of a way that will assist you even more than you considered." You know, you're going to be a day older whether you do anything or not. And if you choose to do something, you can do it either smiling or cursing. But you'll be a whole lot happier if you're smiling; I can guarantee that! If someone is really in a state of cooperation, you can ask him to close a door to keep a room warm, and he will run around and close all the doors, turn up the heat, check the windows and do whatever he can to make sure that you are comfortable. That may be cooperation in an exaggerated way, but it is the willingness to go the extra mile that creates an attitude of cooperation.

When you're living outside cooperation, life can get rather miserable. You may spend a lot of time just sitting around in a state of restlessness, worry or anxiety. The doctors call it ulcers or heartburn. It could also be called heartache, despair, agony and loneliness. You block the flow of energy that is present to be used in action, in DOING. When you block the action, when you don't cooperate with what needs to be done, the energy turns inward and becomes negative, and you move into "down" feelings. Sometimes you curse and blame God for your trouble. God probably didn't have anything to do with it. You do that to yourself. And you can get out of depression by DOING, by moving into the positive flow of action, by cooperating with what is present in your life.

People sometimes feel that life is unfair, and they

don't deserve the things that happen to them. But it's just not so. When you cry out, "Why me, Lord?" the reply might very well be, "Because you promoted it, it's coming to you; and I love you so much that I'll allow you to experience and learn from your own creation." You always get the things you have worked to create, and that applies equally to things positive and negative. You get the return in proportion to the effort that you put forth — physically, emotionally, mentally and spiritually. We are creators, and we are very adept at it. So when something happens in your life that you either like or dislike, take a look at what you did to bring it to yourself.

There are a few quick ways to know when you're not in a state of cooperation. One is the attitude of, "I'm right!" This attitude creates separation because it places a judgment on someone or something else. Another key to knowing you're not cooperating is the attitude of, "You're wrong!" As soon as you hear yourself say that, get somebody to kick you real hard where it hurts to wake you up and get you to look at your attitude. Another way to know you're not cooperating is when you hear yourself say, "Yes, but...." The way to cooperate with people who are expressing these negative attitudes is to let them win, to let them have their way. It's easy. When they've won, you can continue in your own positive direction without becoming involved in their point of view at all.

We're moving into the New Age, the Golden Age, an age where the awareness of Spirit is present more completely than ever before. People are learning and growing at a tremendous rate. You'll be faced continually with opportunities for cooperation. You may be aware of and be able to move into some of them, and you may miss others. But later, if your energy drops out from under you and you start to feel the "down" feelings, you may realize you missed a chance for self-cooperation. Use those times to teach you. Look back at those situations and evaluate where you moved out of cooperation and into the personal point of view of, "I'm right." Then look for the next opportunity to cooperate and to practice the positive attitude.

People who deal in levels of false expectation often find it difficult to work in a high degree of cooperation. When you enter into an expectation that someone will behave a certain way or a situation will turn out a certain way or you will get a certain result from your action — and that expectation turns out to be false — you often find yourself expressing disappointment, unhappiness, despair or depression....depending on your emotional investment in the outcome. Expectation is a good area to stay away from. When you just let others be and cooperate with what is, you find your life flowing along much more smoothly and happily.

Many people expect me to be very different from what I am. They have a particular image of me in their minds, and when they meet me for the first time, they often say, "I expected you to be a man about fifty or sixty years old with long hair and a beard — but you're not that at all." I say, "You're right." It's almost as though they think I should defend the fact that I do not fit their expectation, that I should soothe their false expectation.

When people have false expectations, there is nothing you can do for them. They have to handle it themselves. If you try to make amends and bridge the gap between their false expectations and the reality of what is, you'll find yourself becoming caught in something unpleasant. Let me give you an example: You go to a movie, enjoy it and tell your friends about it. Then they go to the movie, and their expectation level is so high based on your description, that the movie is a flop for them. So they come back to you and say, "You recommended **that** movie?" You say, "Yes, right, didn't you think it was great?" They say, "No, we thought it was lousy." You say, "But didn't you like the part when....?" and you immediately start defending your opinion.

If people are disappointed as a result of a false expectation, the feeling is theirs to handle. If you talk about the Light or MSIA and people create illusions and disappointments about it, you're not bound to defend your position. You don't have to defend anything because they're free to come and go, and that's the only level of honesty in which you can work. If you try to defend against their illusions, can you see the problem you will have ? You may have to come to the point where you sound rude by saying, "Suit yourself." If they come to an attitude of cooperation and are willing to hear your point of view, then you can continue the relationship. In other words, if they drop their expectations and allow you to do what you can do, you are free to relate to them. If they lift in consciousness, you both can be joyful. And if they don't lift, you can both be clear in consciousness. Either way you're in pretty good territory.

If you want to live a more balanced and happy life, accept the following challenge. If someone says, "Oh, I thought that should have been done better," just say, "That's an interesting point of view," and go on about your business. When you feel you have to "sell" them — don't; just go on about your business. People sell themselves. You can give them the opportunity to do that, however. Present your particular service or idea and explain what it can do for them if they use it the way it's designed to be used. If they use it another way and it doesn't work, you are not responsible.

It's best to stay clear and free in your consciousness, to know where you are, what you're doing and what your approach is. Then if people start interpreting what you do and making it into something else, you can simply tell them, "Suit yourself," and step away into your own direction. When you allow them the freedom to suit themselves and go on with their direction, and when you make it clear that you're going to continue working the way you're working, it becomes a great security for everyone. When

116

you say, "I won't allow you to interfere with what I'm doing, and I'm not going to interfere with what you're doing," you will find great respect coming to you — not necessarily admiration or glorification, but respect.

Moving Into Oneness

Spirituality is a very simple way of life. It is not complex at all. The simplicity of the consciousness of spiritually aware people makes it very easy for them to go into the primordial consciousness of Spirit and allow it to be. The complexity is the expectation people place on it and the levels of illusion people project into it. Because the spiritual form is so simple and pure, it's malleable; it can be molded into anything. It allows itself to be molded into various levels of consciousness.

You can, in a very simple way, reach into the spiritual consciousness by just saying, "Here I am, Father. I'll follow whatever direction you lead." You just let the Light and the Spirit flow in; that's the most simple way. It is also the most direct way and the most complete way. For some it may be the most difficult and frustrating way because not too many people are going to let go and let anything come in. They're going to reach out and try to yank it in, or attempt to control and create all sorts of things and then force other people into their mold. Yet you know that when other people attempt to force **you** into their mold and when they think they've won, you file for divorce or leave your job because you don't fit their mold.

On the mental level, you often play all sorts of games, attempting to defend yourself and your position. But you don't have a vocabulary adequate enough to defend an illusion. It's so much easier to admit an error than to say, "But if the person down the street would have gotten up five minutes earlier and left for work fifteen minutes earlier...." You can use all sorts of excuses, parade the issue and defend your position to make yourself look good, but inside you'll still be miserable because you're not in a balanced state mentally.

I talk to a lot of people, and often when I suggest something to them, they immediately go into a mental defense position: "Don't disturb my mind. I've got my mind made up. Don't give me any new information that might disturb me. I'm settled." You can do anything you want with your mind, if you want to badly enough, but if you're busy defending your position, you really won't be able to do anything very useful with it. It's okay if you feel that you need the defense level; use it until you can get past it. But don't stay in it.

As long as you try to separate yourself from other people, you will have difficulty. This does not mean that you have to reach out and join yourself to them. You're already joined. That oneness is already there. You don't have to do anything, and that's what's so nice. The difficulty comes when you try to separate yourself from other people by saying, "Who needs you?" A little voice inside says, "Me." Then you think, "Well, I can hold out longer than they can." So you back off, then **they** back off, and it's miserable because you didn't want them to back off. You wanted them to turn around and say, "Oh, I'm sorry," and come forward and beg forgiveness. But they expected **you** to do the same thing, so it's a standoff. It seems nobody is going to move.

You may say, "I don't see you coming forward and saying it was your fault." They may say, "No, because it was really your fault." So more separation takes place. It's much easier to say, "If you think it was my fault, maybe you could show me how to correct it. The way you see it, what is it that I'm supposed to do?" That point of view can become very lifting. And if you are really smart, you might add, "It probably was my fault." That simple statement will likely correct the imbalance. Saying you're sorry doesn't necessarily reestablish communication, but it does

119

stop the outer push that is attempting separation. And underneath, it is still together.

Even though we have different corporal bodies, there is still a oneness among these bodies. We are still connected together. You might wonder how this can be. Yet you can walk into a room where somebody has a headache, sit by them and start experiencing their headache. You might turn around and ask, "Do you have a headache?" They respond, "Yes." You say, "I've got it, too!" There is a connection among physical bodies.

We seem to be very much connected in our emotions. I fully realized this fact one night when I saw a movie showing Indians being massacred — men, women and children. To express their grief and pain, they threw dirt in the air. I thought, "We don't throw dirt in the air physically, but we do it in other ways." There is something very real and right about expressing the emotional hurt this way, about getting into the dirt where you can release the frustrations and start moving your body around. Sometimes it seems we're not that smart these days. We might hit someone in the nose instead of going back to some of these old rituals that are universal, workable ideas. Getting down to the dirt level and throwing things around on that level releases the emotions without inflicting hurt on anyone else.

Sometimes when you're really hitting someone hard and you think you're not hurting them, you hit even harder at them to get in. Often you're already in much too far and stomping much too hard, and the other person is doing everything he can to get away from you. The person may be backing off so fast emotionally that you experience even greater pain. When people hit you too hard emotionally, just tell them, "I understand what's happening. I can feel what you're going through. You don't have to stomp any longer; I can feel it. You don't have to yell; I can hear you. You're in. Now let's come into a calmness and solve the problem.''

It takes quite a bit of wisdom to tell a person, ''You're in on the level of my hurt. You're in an area that's going to hurt me, and I'm going to be shutting myself off to you. That could mean I'm going to shut myself in, and lest I do that, I'm going to express myself with someone else.'' If you don't let the emotions flow in some direction, you can become locked in. If someone can't understand you intellectually, find people that can relate to you on a mental level. If you're on an emotional level, find people that can relate to you emotionally. You can flow with these different levels where you can work, relate and grow.

Most of us have had just about too much separation and hurt, so we're moving into the ultimate level of conscious spiritual awareness. We flow toward those people seeking the same thing so we don't lock ourselves away from the rest of the world. As we progress in our awareness of ourselves, we can help each other move through the levels of hurt and despair into the joy of accomplishing. We start having the courage and the ability to speak up very carefully and tell other people what our responsibilities are and are not.

To be spiritually aware is not necessarily to be ''wishy-washy.'' Spiritually aware people have hope, charity and kindness — which is sometimes mistaken for weakness. But spiritually aware people are strong because it takes great strength to break away from the people who would pull you into the muck and mire where they are. You may have to say, ''I love you, and I never thought I could exist without you, but I am now going to do that.'' If they say, ''There must be something terrible happening; you're pulling away from me,'' you can say, ''I'm not **pulling** away from you; you are **pushing** me away.''

You may come together with another human being and say, ''We can walk together and share what we can share.

121

If we can talk about herbs as a common meeting ground, that is the level on which we will share." There may be special loves with whom you want to share on more levels in order to move into a greater union of oneness and greater spiritual love. You may become a "dynamo" as you allow the greater energy of Spirit to be transformed down through your consciousness and out into the rest of the world to all other levels.

The Holy Spirit will use you when you clear yourself to allow it to flow into your consciousness and out into the other levels. Many times when you're not sure what to do in a certain situation, you can just ask for the Light "for the highest good of all concerned," and the Holy Spirit can then flow through you in whatever way is clear. You then walk in a divine consciousness that says, "Whatever happens is okay."

If you shake people, it is just possible that is what is needed for them at this time and that you are the one bringing in the Spirit which will allow them to grow into a greater awareness, to clear out whatever has been blocking them. If something you hear or see shakes you, whether it's physical, emotional or mental, **that** is your area at which to look because it may be blocking you from reaching your Self. Go at it with a great devotion and fervor. Don't give in until you can handle the situation in a neutral conscious-ness — not just a capable or competent one, but a masterful one. Then it's easy to master the second and third area because they're already in line to be mastered. Mastering that first one can be really rough. After that it's easier.

The truths are all universal. "Seek ye first the kingdom of God" is really the most profound message I can utter to you. **Seek ye first the kingdom of God. The kingdom of God is within. The Father resides in His heaven. You are that spiritual being that you have been waiting for. You are the Promised One.** That Spirit that is

you reaches out into the world to make things work. That's why, when you reach out to other people or teachers, you have a difficult time making your life work. You, yourself, are the Promised One. That is not outside of yourself. It does not reside in anyone outside of you. You have to reach into your Self to make your life work.

In this New Age, you have infinite opportunity to move into the higher qualities. Keep enthusiasm present in all your activities. Anticipate joy at every moment. And always maintain a sense of being grateful for all of your blessings. Being grateful means maintaining the aware-ness that God is entirely present in every moment of your life and that you don't have to go anywhere to experience the glory of God's presence. When you are in that type of awareness and cooperation, all things flow to you, and you experience a sense of upliftment and peace. The joy of it is that you can turn to the positive direction at any moment and the joy will be entirely present for you.

When the joy of Spirit is present, you can't do enough good works. Your cooperation is full. Your love is manifest. Your Light shines forth into the world. You become of service to everyone you meet. You spread the Light consciousness everywhere you go. Your mere presence brings balance and joy to people. And you don't even have to say a word. The Light will move through you to others and bring them what is necessary and beneficial. To live in grace and maintain your awareness of the Spirit within is a beautiful service. If you do nothing but that, you are a Light unto this world.

As you consciously
lift into the level of
Soul, you move into a
clearer expression
of responsibility.

You Are Your Responsibility

Chapter Six

You are a lot more, as a friend of mine once said, than that "bag of bones" you carry around with you. The indwelling consciousness of God, through the Soul, uses the physical body for its expression on this planet. And that makes the human being very special. The consciousness of God is present with everyone. The Spirit is present with everyone. Spirit flows, though differently, through cigarette smokers, marijuana smokers, alcoholics, Coca-Cola drinkers, milk drinkers, meat eaters, vegetarians, fruitarians and people who just fast for long periods of time. However, the same Spirit is present in all. And God consciousness floods through each one. If you could put one thought in your mind and keep it there continually, you'd find yourself gazing upon the face of God, and that one thought would be: **God is.**

Everything that exists is part of God. Everything has life and movement. In some parts of God there is more realization of that Godself than in other parts. A cat has more awareness than a rock; a man, more than a cat. But when perceived through advanced scientific instruments, even those things that appear to be inanimate are seen to be made up of particles in motion.

Sometimes a "sense" that you cannot readily perceive with the physical senses, you label as "no sense" or nonsense. And you dismiss it as not worth paying attention to.

Much of your responsibility on this physical planet is to **listen** to what is being said to you, pay attention to who says it, and then work the information you have been given. If it works for you, use it. Make it a part of your approach to life. If it doesn't work for you, let it go. Or put it aside until later when it might be more usable to you. When you hear something that appears to you to be nonsense, you don't have to label it nonsense or bad or evil or anything like that. You simply see that it isn't relevant to your position at this time. And you keep yourself open to the possibility that the person who gave you that information might be seeing life from a perspective very different from yours. It doesn't have to be categorized as normal or abnormal, average or strange, or anything else.

Often you try to get other people to be exactly like you. You label, categorize and pigeonhole so you can get your universe neatly under your control and do with it whatever you want. "Normal" people sometimes allow this to happen. Abnormal people may say, "Hey, I can't breathe your air and digest your food. You have to do that yourself. And I will breathe and digest however I feel like doing it." Now, that's abnormal. Or is it normal?

More people are learning to take responsibility for their own actions. It becomes more and more difficult to lay your troubles at somebody else's doorstep and say, "My misery is your fault." No, your misery is only your choice. Your joy is also your choice. Those choices and all the variables between are available to you at any moment. Too often, you allow the temporary feeling state of the body to misrepresent who you are inside. If you have a headache, you might appear to be a little short-tempered and sharp. If you have an upset stomach, you might appear to be grouchy and grumpy. And if you don't get eight hours of sleep one night, the next day you might appear irritable and angry. The same body, when it's rested and feeling well, may be very loving, tender, caring and open to the world. Which are you? Which is real? Might it be possible

126

to override the temporary states of imbalance in the body or the emotions and continue to express the loving being you are?

If you were to look at your life and its expression from a high consciousness, you would see that there is no necessity for judgment. Move your perception out of the **imagination.** Your life is not what you imagine it to be. Move your perception out of the **emotions.** Your life is not what you feel it to be. You know that because you can feel awful, then get a phone call from your best friend and feel wonderful, all in the space of a few moments. So your life is not your emotions. Move your perception above the **mental** level. Your life is not your thoughts. You think all sorts of things; if your life were your every thought, you'd probably be in a state of confusion. Move your perception up through the unconscious, **etheric** realm. As you get your perception high enough, you see that things just are.

Your life is what it is. Whatever your expression, it's all right because it is an expression of your awareness. If you smoke, that doesn't mean you're evil. It means that expression is satisfying something within you at some level. When you find a different way to satisfy and fulfill that something, you might not be smoking anymore. You don't have to judge yourself for what appears to be negative expression. **And** you can pay attention and look for expressions that will more comfortably and more nearly express the inner self you know yourself to be.

You never turn completely from the Light into the darkness. You can turn to a lesser degree of Light, a Light expression less than what is possible for you. And when you do that, you might see a lot of shadows and it might be a little dark and murky. There is Light, however, in all extensions of God in all universes. The mind, the body, the words, the emotions are so very far from perfect it's sometimes a wonder that we get the body out of bed in the morning and safely back there at night. If that doesn't

127

require a form of God consciousness, I don't know what does.

So many times you've said, "Oh, God, I'll never get through this. I can't handle this. I'll never live through this." But you do. You lied to yourself because you are here. You might just as well own up to the fact that you're going to keep right on living your life however you create it for yourself. You're going to keep right on going through the things necessary for your growth and upliftment. You're going to keep right on handling what you bring forward for yourself. You're going to continue expressing the God consciousness you are, moving to a more and more perfect expression of the God within. That's just the way it is.

Checking
It Out

o you know the difference between an optimist and a pessimist? The story is told of two little boys who were put into two rooms piled high with manure. A couple of hours went by, and someone checked on the two boys. One was crying and complaining about the sight and the smell of the manure and his "horrible" fate at being shut up in the room. The other little boy was smiling with great joy and shoveling manure just as fast as he could. When asked why he looked so happy, he said, "With all this manure, there's got to be a pony around here someplace."

Those of us who are optimists recognize that the next good thing is always coming our way. If you want to be an optimist, if you want your energies to be lifting, if you want to realize your highest potential for joy and fulfillment, then you must pledge to yourself that, from this moment, you will become more and more aware of what you are doing **now**.

When you live in the **now**, you can bring yourself into full awareness of the moment. You bring yourself into awareness of your body. Should you be hanging up your clothes? If so, move your physical body to hang them up **now**. If you don't, an hour later they will still be there, waiting to be done **now**.

Perhaps you have prayed for a better job. Maybe you can't have that because your sloppiness is blocking you. If you can't adequately handle your responsibilities **now,** how can you hope to handle greater responsibilities? So be aware of the responsibilities you have physically and fulfill those. Prepare yourself physically to complete what you say you will complete.

As you increase your awareness of **now**, look at the level of your emotions. You have no responsibility to past feelings or probable future feelings. Your responsibility is to **now**. All you need to do is accept your emotions in the moment, work within that present structure, and continually let go and move freely to the next moment. This method automatically handles past feelings as you always keep yourself up-to-date. It's all **now**. No moment of awareness is not **now**.

The next level on which to focus your awareness is the level of the mind. What thoughts are you having **now**? Where are they leading you?

To achieve an action that is fulfilling, that leads to joy, you need a **match** in thoughts, feelings, and physical response. When those three areas match, you **act**, and the result is success. Failure often results if you attempt to act when all three areas are not in harmony. For example, in your inner dialogue, your mind may say, "This seems right to do." But if you **act** based upon the thought alone, you may find yourself isolated in your ivory tower someplace, holding back the things you don't want to handle — putting out intellectual statements to justify your position, while feeling very insecure about the validity of that position.

A thought without a feeling is half-alive. For instance, if a thought comes to you — "It would be a good idea to go back to school and get my degree" — check out the feeling level. You must have a feeling to match that thought. If you're happy with your job and your present life style, you may find that the thought of going back to school creates funny feelings, maybe a little doubt, maybe a great deal of "butterflies" in the stomach. You could change the thought a little — "It would be a good idea to take a leave of absence from my job in six months and go back to

130

school." Check to see how that feels. "That feels better!" In six months, you check with your boss about the leave of absence, check out the present feeling level, and you may find that you **now** feel very good about going back to school. So you have a thought and a feeling to match it. Then you check out the physical level. The body says, "I can handle that change in lifestyle — in fact, it might be fun." Now there is a match of thought, feeling and the physical response. And the action will probably be a clear one. You also have to consider Spirit, and if all the other levels say "clear," it's generally clear with Spirit.

When you've checked all your levels, found them "clear" and then moved on your decision, you may still have people come to you and say, "You stupid idiot, do you know what you've done!?" And your answer can very clearly be, "Yes, I know what I've done. I thought about it for six months, felt about it for four weeks, moved on it physically, completed the new pattern, and I'm clear with the action." If they say, "Do you know you're causing concern for a lot of people?" your response might be, "No, I didn't know that, but if people have concern, I will handle that as they bring it to me." That way you remain true to yourself and your action; you remain responsible for yourself.

Once you act thoughtfully and in your fullest awareness, you are clearer. And if there are repercussions, you take responsibility for them and move on. That's all you can do. There is no reason to feel uptight or guilty about any action you undertake if you have checked it out first and moved into it in awareness. You do what you can do based upon what you know, based upon what you feel, based upon where you are. And then you let it go and go on from there.

Living in the **now** means that you are involved in a continual process of receiving and integrating new information, of recognizing new and changing emotional

131

states, of shifting physical states and of making new decisions based upon new responses. You work the new wisdoms. You modify your behavior. You bring your experience forward, snap into gear and move forward in your **success.**

You may find yourself letting go of what has been. You focus on what is. You cannot have your mind **back there** in failure thoughts. You cannot have your mind **back there** in success thoughts. Either way, if you're **back there** trying to live in the past, you are manifesting your lack of awareness of the present moment.

When you are building your dream one brick at a time, you put each brick down and go get the next brick. You don't stand still for twenty-four hours looking at the last brick you laid. In twenty-four hours you could have built the whole wall.

The process of **now** is the process of Spirit, the process of Soul. Those who are traveling the spiritual path as taught by the Mystical Traveler, through MSIA, are going into Soul, into what is greater and higher, what is more dignified, more ethical.

The higher people go in the spiritual flow, the more ethical they become in their relationships with themselves and with others. Integrity results and integration is so fulfilling. Sometimes people can mistake the **ethics** of a spiritual person for weakness and think, ''I can go ahead and do what I want because I can just stomp all over you.'' They may find out that they've stomped on an atomic bomb. Then they walk around confused, hurt, psychologically out of balance with themselves, socially out of balance with others, and personally out of balance with their families.

When you feel like telling someone off, check all your levels. Is the response emotional? If it is, check to see if there is an intellect behind it, a logical, valid reason for your upset — not a trumped-up reason to justify the emotions. If there is an emotional response and a valid reason, check the results of a physical response. If that also reads "clear," present your point of view in the awareness that you will be responsible for the result. If you do all that, you'll be clear.

If you give up your awareness of **now**, if you act without having a **match** in your thoughts, emotions, and your physical actions, you can throw yourself into great disturbance. If you tell off another person when you could have been quiet and held a Light consciousness for them, you bring disturbance to yourself.

When you do not maintain your awareness of and your responsibility to the **now**, the present moment, you separate yourself from your reality. And in that separation, you can create your own hell. Then you know your Soul only by the reflection of those who know the Soul, rather than through your own direct experience of the Soul.

The consciousness can enter into patterns of extreme irresponsibility that separate it from its own reality, its knowledge of God, and create a living hell. Abuse of any negative pattern can result in separation.

# Educating
Your Self

Years ago I was working with a young student, introducing him to the idea that more is going on than can be perceived from the physical level. In a way, he was somewhat aware of other levels because he'd introduced himself to drugs a year or two earlier.

One morning after taking an acid trip, he came in to see me. I saw that he had picked up an entity, an elemental form of consciousness possessing intelligence but lacking a body through which to express itself. He said, "I tripped out last night." I said, "Yes, I know you did." He said, "Man, I really flipped out." I said, "What did you do? Take acid?" He said, "Yeah. Really up, man, really up." I said, "So?" He said, "I'm not back." I said, "I know you're not back, and what's more, you've got company." He said, "I know it. I've got something with me, haven't I?" I said, "Yes." This was a fearful thing for a boy who had trouble spelling his first name. He said, "I never thought this type of thing would happen to me." That's what **everybody** says.

What happened was that he had given up his responsibilities to his own body. He was abusing it, not taking care of it. He was taking these drug-induced "trips" more or less regularly. His consciousness would take off into other realms and leave the body open to whatever came along.

The young man asked, "What am I going to do now?" I said, "Well, a few things can happen. One is that this entity can go away. But it's there; it has come in, so it's not really going to be too anxious to leave. So another possible action is that it's going to stay right where it is. And the third possibility is that it can take you over. It can possess you, and then you will be under its control and not under your own control."

You might wonder how this type of thing could happen under God's will and divine law. It could happen because the boy gave up his responsibility and his right to that body. That body is also a part of God's will and divine law. **You** are your responsibility — right down to the level of your physical body. It's been said, "To thine own self be true." This idea is important. You can't give up your responsibility to any outside agent. The outside agents, in this instance, happened to be acid, marijuana, pills, glue and other drugs.

So the boy asked, "What's going to happen to me?" I said, "This form which is with you will probably back off its pressure. It will back off so that it won't be obvious to you, so that you won't know it's there. Then it will push you into the desire pattern to take acid again. It will create the feeling that, 'Oh, it was just one of those things. You're okay now; don't worry about it.' And it will continue to urge you into drug involvement which will cause you to release direction over your consciousness. It will keep moving in a little bit more until it becomes the assertive pattern, and then it will just do everything it can to get rid of you."

In this action of an entity coming in and taking over a body, the original consciousness can be pushed out. In this case, the boy's consciousness could have been separated from his body; his consciousness could have been pulled away from it. Because he had karma with that body, if he separated his consciousness prematurely, he would not be able to go to any other body or any other dimension. He would be earthbound. He would not be able to do anything except hang around close to the body and cry out woefully into darkness. There would be nothing there but darkness. He would not be able to progress in a natural evolvement of his consciousness and his Spirit. Then, at the time his body died, his consciousness would be released to travel on to the realm he had to reach to fulfill his karma. And that, of course, would be okay. Ultimately, either way is okay. One way takes much longer than the other and may be **more difficult** for the consciousness to handle.

We talked about his responsibility to himself, and he said, "Okay, I understand. I won't take acid anymore. I know what's going on. I understand." I said, "You really don't know what's going on yet, because you have been told before that this type of action was coming toward you. It was suggested before that you stay clear of drugs because of the possibility that you could lose control of yourself." He had heard the words, but did not yet have the understanding.

The entity could have been taken off, forced out very rapidly with the Light and the power of Spirit. But unless he educated his consciousness, that gap would reappear, and he would go into the same or similar patterns all over again. This is why the Bible says that when you take off an entity, seven more can come in its place. The consciousness has to change so that it can hold its direction and not allow the entity form to take control.

The boy knew when the entity came in. He said, "It scared me so badly!" And then he used some very profane words he didn't usually use. Then he said, "See. Like that — **like that!**" I just looked at him. Some other people came in and heard the profanity. They looked at him and said, "Hey, what happened to you?" They were aware that the Light was not strong with him, that something was wrong, something was different. I could **see** the entity that was with him; they **sensed** that something was different.

It's important to recognize that the entity that came in felt within its rights to take over this body, to complete some things necessary to its own evolvement, because the

136

boy, by his action and irresponsibility, was giving up the body. The entity had looked in on the drug pattern, tapped into the consciousness and then when the consciousness was away, when it left the body unprotected, the entity moved in.

I worked with the boy a little bit that morning, bringing the Light in very quietly, just to stabilize him, but not to push the entity off. As things were explained to him, he got quite scared and resolved not to go into the drug experience ever again. But he came back after lunch and said, "Hey, the entity is gone." I said, "How's that?" He said, "I don't feel it there. It's gone." I said, "It's not gone." He said, "I knew it wasn't. It's tricking me. I thought it was gone, and I was going to smoke some marijuana. I think I could do that and get away with it anyway. I can, can't I?" I said, "Suit yourself. You know what the entity's aim is. It was explained to you. Nothing's changed. Just because you've changed your mind doesn't mean that it has changed its mind. It's there; it's going to stay there. You have to watch it."

He was told that, from this time on, he couldn't do anything that would give over any of his consciousness, his conscious direction, to anything outside — not smoke a cigarette or have a beer or anything. I said, "You can't even allow your friends to lead you into a decision. If you make a wrong decision, at least it's yours. You must assert your right to decide, right or wrong. If they say, 'Let's cut class,' and you take off, that's the same as giving yourself over to the acid, because you are giving up your control." So he went to classes that day. Later he said, "I knew it was right down to the 'nitty-gritty,' and I had to do something." He knew that this **giving in** process was part of what he had to overcome in his life pattern.

That night, I spent some time projecting the Light his way, sending it for his highest good. He came in the next morning looking so much better. The entity was pushed

137

way out, but it was still hanging around. He told me, "Last night I was thinking about you and the things you've told me. I got really angry because I knew you could take the entity away, and you wouldn't do it. But all of a sudden, I just sat down like you've told me to do, and I concentrated on you and thought, 'I know you can take this thing away, so just do it!' And something came all through my room and all around me, and I started feeling so much better." I said, "That was the Light being sent your way." He wasn't too sure of what to do next so I just said, "Keep breathing in and breathing out," and he agreed to do that.

It was important to educate his consciousness, to explain to him what was happening, to let him know the things that he could do to prevent this type of action from happening. It was important to explain to him the habit patterns that he had established within himself and where these were leading him. And at that time it was important to not remove the entity from him, but to show him how he could remove the entity from himself by educating himself, by assuming responsibility for himself and his actions and by taking care of himself. It's easy to give in; it's easy to give up your rights and your consciousness. But later, you have to come around and look at the responsibility levels and do something about them. When you can assume the responsibility of yourself and overcome the tests that come your way, when you can learn from the experiences that are presented to you, you can be lifted very high in consciousness and greatly enhance your spiritual growth.

Evaluating Your Information

Irresponsibility may manifest as abuse of any negative pattern. Drinking too much leads to giving up conscious control of your life and avoiding responsibility for yourself. Over-dependency on another human being—a spouse, a lover, a child, a parent—can create a tendency toward giving up responsibility for yourself. The example of drug abuse is a very obvious one. Often you deal with levels of irresponsibility that are very subtle. It is a wise approach to maintain control of your life, your choices and your decisions. Ultimately you are the only one who can decide the course of your life; and you are the only one responsible. Don't attempt to get someone else to make your decisions for you. You have to learn to read the signals your universe gives you. Learn to observe and select. It's called discernment.

Sometimes you may feel incapable of sorting through all the data coming in to make a sensible decision. But what's your choice? Is your choice to give over your responsibility to someone else? It's like going into a big computer firm and asking a question of the computer — after the due process of time, perhaps thirty seconds, out comes a punched card that has the answer within it. The computer expert hands it to you and says, "There is your answer." You look at it and say, "Wow! Holes punched in a card," because that's all you can perceive. That's your physical vision.

If you get someone who is trained to read the card, they might say, "It says this and this and this." You look at it and say, "How could you get all that information out of a few holes punched in a card?" The expert may offer to teach you how to read it and show you a few simple codes.

The next day you go back and ask another question of the computer. It gives you another card. You try to read it and say, "The holes are in different places. I can't read this card. But I can read yesterday's card." So your computer teacher says, "All right, read the one you read yesterday." So you read that one pretty well, but you make a few mistakes. The teacher corrects your mistakes and tells you what the correct meaning is. You say, "Oh, right! I forgot. I didn't take good mental notes and didn't look at it after I went home. I really didn't do my homework, so I'm not sure about the answers. It sounded so simple when you told me about it yesterday." So the teacher says, "Let me show you how to read the second card," and explains that one to you. You say, "Oh, I can see that. I see how that fits in with the first one. That makes sense."

The next day you come back with another question; thirty seconds later, out comes another card with more holes in it, and they're different holes again. But now maybe you're starting to see a pattern. You say, "This hole is like the other one. That's the letter 'F' there. Right?" And your teacher may say, "Right." You say, "Hurrah! I'm growing because I got an 'F' out of all the letters." And your teacher explains to you what's going on, how you can take your cards home and study the coding so that when the next card comes out, you can take it home and, through arduous work, decode the holes in that card. Soon you would be able to read the cards yourself, without assistance. That is being responsible for your own growth.

The same process exists in the spiritual quest. You must become responsible for your spiritual growth. Prior to that time, you are relying upon someone else. You may get very disgusted and say, "Why can't I read the holes on the card? Why can't I do it?" Your teacher may say, "If we kept running the same card through each time, you could. But we have to make modifications each time to take care of certain progressions that the computer is making." This really relates to the reincarnation patterns that each person goes through. If you come back enough times as that one card, as that one consciousness, you learn to read that one pretty well. And you say, "Hurrah! I can read this pattern. I can handle this." After you have worked enough patterns, you have many, many more answers than the person who doesn't even know the computer exists, not to mention that it's shooting out these cards over and over again.

You may pick up a computer card and say, "Oh, I don't know what this says." So you ask someone else what it says, and that person answers, "It says such and such and such." He hands it to you, and you say, "All right. If you say that's it, that must be it." Then along come others who ask about the meaning on their cards, and this same person answers in a very similar way — and all of a sudden you realize the new person has his own "decoding device" where all cards are read just about the same way. That is pretty much how orthodox religion started coming into our lives. No matter what the holes were, it got read the same way.

Later you happen to be with someone who works with the computer, and they say, "Oh, they had the first fourteen letters right, absolutely right — but these other forty-five letters have been read incorrectly. You've been given inaccurate information." Then the programmer may say, "I'll give you a card, and we'll punch it on this machine so you can look at it as it's punched. Now you have the accurate information. Take it to the person who has been reading the cards for you, and ask him to read this one to you. You know how it is punched, so you can see how accurately he reads it. You will be able to reevaluate how accurate his total observation is."

This reevaluation process is what's going on now in many religions around the world. It is a time to reevaluate. When you actually start reading the card yourself, you are

141

finding out that things you have been told over and over and over were not read accurately enough for you. When you are responsible for yourself, you rely on your own knowledge, your own experience — you begin to read the cards for yourself. Yes, you may read some incorrectly, but you keep going and learning and increasing your ability.

It is not the fault of those who read the cards to you that the information is inaccurate. It's not the fault of religions or religious men. The fault, if any, is that you don't read the cards yourself — that is **your** responsibility. It's so easy to shift responsibility off to other people and say, "Well, it's their fault." Remember, no matter how much you point your finger at someone else, three fingers point back at you. So you have to be very careful about trying to blame or judge. Ultimately, you are responsible for yourself.

As you grow into greater levels of responsibility, you perceive a maturing quality within yourself. As you rely on yourself and do not look "out there" for total validation and approval, you discover a growing sense of "self" within you. That is the stirring of the Soul, awakening to its own greater nature. As you consciously lift into the level of Soul, you move into a clearer expression of responsibility, you see more of the Light, you find it easier to reach beyond the levels of mind, body, and emotions; you **know** yourself more clearly and purely.

When you are in the Soul, you can see more easily the pitfalls and the obstacles of your life on these lower levels. You can experience a love for and a oneness with other people that is beyond anything you've experienced before. The way to learn about the Soul is to be open to the possibility that it exists; accept the possibility you are more than your body, your thoughts, or your feelings. You don't have to believe it. You don't have to have faith. Just be open to the possibility that it exists. Soon more information will start coming in to you. You might bring back memory of a dream, tell someone about it and find out they had the same dream. You might be having difficulty making a decision, and in a moment of quiet contemplation, see the decision made and even experience the result of your choice — and come back **knowing** which way to move. You might suddenly find yourself in two locations simultaneously and know that you are experiencing Soul transcendence.

These things could represent only the beginning of your experience of Soul. There is so much there for you once you open yourself to it and place yourself upon this path of unfoldment. It's magnificent. And it is all a manifestation of **love**. Love is the matrix that makes it all possible; it is the energy of Spirit that is the essence. And it is through love for yourself that you find the Soul and learn that its expression is your reality.

There is only one Soul, and that is God. There is only one love, and that is God. There is only one intellect, and that is God. There is only one, which is God. We are manifestations of God, on whatever level we choose to express.

I'm called the Mystical Traveler, but I answer to every name and every form. The Traveler is a form that you cannot restrict. It's totally free and totally of the moment. Because it is free and of the moment, it creates health, wealth and happiness in the physical world. The Mystical Traveler **is** that and needs nothing more than what it is. The Traveler shares all that with you, freely, from Spirit. The Traveler gives to you the keys to unlock your own health, wealth and happiness. You must receive the keys each moment, for they are different each moment.

The presence of God is inside of you, manifesting anew every moment. It is not your emotions, your mind, or your physical body. It is Spirit — expressing through those levels, but always more than that. You sit right on the edge of Soul awareness. It's so close. It's there each moment.

Each moment gives you new opportunity to discover that awareness.

When you live in the moment and live free, you're living in Soul. Let go of each moment as it passes. Detach yourself from this earth, from memories of the past, from expectations of the future. Do those things that bring you health, wealth and happiness in a detached state and let all the rest go.

If you walk among your
fellow men in balance
and grace, you become
a lifting force to every-
one you meet.

Taking Care Of Yourself

Chapter Seven

I'd like to talk a little about "spiritual ecology." This is the ecology of maintaining yourself first — and then the world around you. Spiritually, you have a responsibility to maintain what you have and anything you touch. It is your job to maintain it, because it is all Spirit. Spirit is everywhere; it always has been and always will be.

Spiritual ecology means keeping yourself clean on every level — physically, emotionally, mentally and spiritually. You watch where you place your mind so you don't put out unkind thoughts toward anyone. You watch where you place your emotions so you don't lay heavy trips on anyone. And you watch where you place your words so you don't inadvertently perform "mouth surgery" on anyone. You watch all your inner levels first, and then you watch your outer environment. It may be things like keeping the shoes put away in the closet and the bed made, keeping your car polished and the ashtray cleaned out. Little things can be very important.

You are a universe unto yourself, and you are responsible for yourself. What are you doing with your universe, with your inner beingness? If **God** of the outer world treated you like you treat your own self inwardly, there might be more earthquakes and cataclysms than you could ever imagine.

Because of the things you've created, you may find yourself flooded with so much toxic material that you actually feel sick within your body. That's because of the way you treat yourself — either physically abusing the body, emotionally putting yourself down, mentally confusing yourself or spiritually starving yourself. Treat yourself better. God resides with you in the essence of His Spirit. And you have the responsibility as a cocreator with the God within to keep your own universe clean.

It's easy to see pollution in the outer world. You look around, and there it is. I'm not one who emphasizes the physical world. But it really is time that the Light bearers on the planet, the wayshowers, start shedding the Light of reason and logic everywhere they go. We can leave the physical earth with a much nicer frequency than we found it. These areas of responsibility apply to everyone. One reason the world is in its present condition is because many people "passed the buck" and said, "That doesn't apply to me." Spiritual ecology applies to everyone — **no exceptions.**

Everyone, in every language, of every race, is crying out for the oneness of beingness that is called "God." It has also been called "Christ" and "Buddha" and "Light" and many other things. It isn't necessary to get hung up on the words because it's all One. And when people know this Oneness, the glory of this world will manifest.

It is the responsibility of all of us to take care of what we have, to keep it in good repair and attractive. And when something is no longer useful, it can be changed into a form which will be useful. It's really very simple. It's common sense. And it applies equally to the individual level and to the world level. Pollution is pollution.

If each one of us, at the grass roots level — and that is where we are now — will place our energies of love and Light and understanding into the preservation and maintenance of what we have here, we can move forward into the glory that was once, a long time ago, on this planet earth. We who are here now may not be able to enjoy the total fruition of our labor, but we will know the good for which we are working and preparing. And of course, as we place our consciousness into the Golden Age, we can be there right now. We are the **bridge** in consciousness, and this means that we may sometimes have to get down in the dirt and **work** to get this world back into the consciousness of glory.

Will everyone be able to see the glory when it comes? Spiritually you can perceive anything into which you place your consciousness. The restrictions exist mentally, emotionally and physically. The restrictions show up as a new ache or pain or wrinkle. Maybe you lose some hair, fail an exam or lose your spouse or child; then the hue and cry across the land is, "Woe is me." People cry inwardly when they think they are alone in their experience.

We are all One through Spirit. When you truly realize the Oneness, you know love for yourself and everyone. Then when you see something negative happen, like a lack of understanding or a quarrel, instead of adding fuel to it by saying, "Yes! You were right! You should have hit them over the head," you have a responsibility to place loving and understanding there. Even when someone is fighting and yelling at another, they're really saying, "Please understand me. I can't do it myself. Please listen; I need your help."

It's easy to hear people cry out because they usually let us know their pain, either verbally or by their actions. It's harder to hear Nature crying out. And yet Nature runs through us all. We're a part of that just as we're a part of Spirit. We're part of all things. And we're now experiencing a renaissance, what's known as "back to the earth." It's a positive action — it is increasing our awareness of the gift of our earth and the responsibility we hold for its

149

protection and preservation. The earth is the "Mother-God" and the Father in heaven is the "Father-God." So we pray to the "Father-Mother-God" to give us the loving Light which we need and can give out to all that surrounds us, for the highest good of all concerned.

And yet, it is necessary to keep in mind that perfection is not achieved on the physical level; with the physical body, no one is perfect. In Soul expression, you are already perfect; everyone is. In the consciousness of the body, emotions and mind, you are working to bring yourself into balance so you can more readily see the Soul's perfection. The mind is an avenue that the Soul uses to see itself. It is also the avenue that sees the world for the Soul. This consciousness is the vehicle through which the Soul expresses on this level.

As you learn to keep the physical level balanced, you can move out of the areas of dogma and opinion and move into a state of **being.** In that state, you will be aware of what's going on, but you won't necessarily have to enter into it. You won't have to get down in the "muck and mire" of negative expression. You simply keep yourself balanced and clear within your own consciousness, regardless of what is going on around you. Then from that balanced, stable place, you are able to assist other people much more effectively.

You can do much more for a little baby who is learning to walk by assisting it from a standing position than by lying flat on the floor and trying to lift it from there. You may not be too much help from the floor level. So you stand above the situation and assist where needed. But did you ever see a little baby grabbed by the hand and given a good hard yank up into the air? What did the baby do? Cried and screamed and became frightened, sure. But if you simply put your hand down, the baby can grab hold of your fingers, and you just make sure that you support it, showing it how to wrap its hands around your fingers and hang on to you. And you lift up very slowly, letting it do most of the work. You pull the baby up and let it down, and it'll start striving to come up.

Now that striving may require a lot of effort on the child's part. And not being able to control its bowels too well, it may have an "accident." So you have a messy situation which could be considered imbalanced and negative. But do you stop assisting the child? No, you continue to help it and train it; and one day, when the child learns to stand all by itself, it will also have learned to control the other body movements. It's all part of training and growth and development.

As the youngster gets older, you find out that you have to reach down less and less, because it starts reaching up higher and reaching out more. And one day the child stands up by holding on to some furniture. Then it toddles from one piece of furniture to another. You stand there watching, and you're proud. You may pat the child on the back and say, "You're doing really well. What a good child you are." You'll expand its consciousness for it and give it a new image of itself. The child will accept that new image and start walking further and further with more independence.

This example of training children parallels, in many ways, spiritual growth. It parallels what we call handling "negative expression." Sometimes the situations that we create for ourselves aren't really the nicest in the world, but we still go through them. We always go through them.

I am fortunate to have friends with youngsters and to be considered "family" by these people. Once when I was visiting one of these friends, I started to pick up the baby, and the father said, "Watch how you pick him up." I said, "What's wrong?" He said, "Dirty diapers." I said, "Okay," more to not make the father uncomfortable than from concern on my part. But pretty soon the baby started fussing. And the father became irritated with him because those dirty diapers were staring him right in the face. I said, "Do you want me to change his diapers?" He said, "That's not your job." I said, "Whose job is it?" He said, "Mine." I said, "Then you change him." He changed the baby's diapers, brought the baby back and said, "You know, this is one of the sweetest kids you've ever seen in your life. And he smells so good." Now he could love that baby better because he was really nice and clean. I said, "You mean to tell me you didn't love that baby with dirty diapers?" He said, "I just didn't want to get involved in the situation." I said, "That's your child; you are involved."

The father has two children now and says that things are a lot easier with the second one because at least he knows what to do. He gets busy and handles the situation right away. Then he doesn't have to sit around and wonder when he's going to handle it. He handles things quickly so that the concern doesn't build up. Before, he was denying what was going on, so it just stayed there and seemed to get worse. By recognizing the situation, by placing his consciousness out into that area and handling it, cleaning it up, he now creates balanced situations.

Is that so different from what we do as adults in our spiritual growth? Is it so very different from our lives when we have to clean up our own dirty situations? The way to overcome a dirty situation is to move into it as rapidly as you can and handle it. You can continually keep things as balanced as possible so you don't have to be involved in too much cleaning. Try not making a mess around the house if you don't like to clean. I work to keep things pretty well in line all the time. Something gets out of line every once in a while — we're all in human bodies. But when something goes out of balance, go in and get it back in line as quickly as possible. Or get somebody to help you put it back in line, if necessary.

Much of my work is to help people get things back into line, to show them how they can do it. I show them how to stop doing the things that are hindering their greater expression and help them expand their consciousness — "You're a big boy now. You're a big girl now. Now shoot for higher realms of Light. I'll be right there with you. As you travel from one level of Light to another, I'll be right there. I'll assist you. If you start to fall, I'll lift you. You're not going to bump your head; you won't get hurt."

You are **not** the imbalance of a situation. You are not that bump on the head. You are not that disagreement. You are not that angry explosion. These are just reference points in your progression. You are going **through** these things. You are continually changing the diapers until the baby grows up. You do it because it's your choice. Oh, you can lie in the garbage pile for a long time, but you have to get up and out of it sometime. Either they're going to come and move the garbage out from beneath you, or you're going to get fed up with the way things are and move yourself. You can move out of the garbage much faster by awakening yourself to what's going on.

This awakening is the spiritual inner awareness, perceiving what is reality and continually moving into positive, direct action. The **Movement of Spiritual Inner Awareness** does not retreat from life; it moves through life, teaching you how to handle this level more effectively and keep yourself balanced. Then it shows you a way into the higher levels of Soul awareness.

Identifying
Psychic Influences

I n this physical level, psychic energies are always present, just as spiritual energies are always present. These energies do not function on any type of time line. They are just present, here and now, always, in eternity. "Time" that was ten thousand years ago and "time" that is today are both the same. The energies are always here and now. When you feel psychic energies coming toward you, realize that they may or may not be related to recent events; they could come from actions far distant, in terms of time, but entirely present, in terms of the psychic energy. We're talking about eternity. You might say, "But I don't remember...." Of course not. You're not being required to remember. That "veil of forgetfulness" is part of the process.

Psychic energies can, at times, reach in and attempt to manipulate your mind, your emotions and your body—and can often be very, very effective in doing just that. If you go someplace not under the influence of the psychic energies, someplace positive and uplifting, those negative energies can go with you and create doubt and fear in your consciousness about that positive experience. That negativity can block you from seeking and experiencing positive direction in your life pattern. Those energies can program you to avoid people who can help you. They can bring in thoughts of, "They're bad. They're evil. They'll harm me. They're after my money. They're after my children." And so on.

When you live from your own center, being influenced by psychic energies sounds really farfetched and highly improbable. But if you get involved in psychic meetings where you are subjected to emotional influences, it **can** happen. People who deal in psychic energy may harangue and harass you with emotionally-laden statements. For example, they may tell you someone or some group is evil, bad, wicked, and you'll be ready to go hunt them down. Something inside of you really shakes; you find yourself really caught up in the group energy, and you think, "They're right!"

Years ago when the Watts riots took place in Los Angeles, much of this process was happening. The psychic energy was loose, and it was manipulating people in unbelievable ways. People who would probably never behave violently within their own life expression were rioting, fighting and looting. A psychic energy was taking over, and it ran its course. This only explains what was going on; it does not excuse the action.

Once, when some riots in the Boston area had recently happened, I was traveling through there. I could feel where people had been fighting, where the energy was close to the energy that kills. The energy force of the violence was palpable. Yet physically, it was a beautiful, clear, brisk day. Part of my job, when I become aware of these "psychic attacks," is to clear that energy, to alter, transmute or change it from the heavy influence of negativity to the positive influence of spiritual energy. It can be changed. But it means recognizing the nature of the psychic attack, maintaining the integrity of your behavior in spite of the psychic energies and then bringing the spiritual essence into that space.

People get caught up in the influence of psychic energies because of something within them that seeks for power or seeks to be recognized as "God." It is that assertiveness for the individual power that causes one to fall out of grace and leaves the person open for the psychic powers to attack. The attack comes to that area which is weakest, most vulnerable, most open to influence.

155

The sexual area, perhaps more than other areas, is one that is very open to the manipulation of psychic energies, because the sexual energy is, of itself, so intense that it creates a ready channel for psychic power to enter. In this sense, the symbology of the Adam and Eve story has great validity. Adam and Eve walked naked among themselves, and in their own purity, they did not need clothing. Yet when the psychic power, the negative energies, entered into their expression, the sexual areas were corrupted, and they covered themselves. When the psychic power comes in with the sexual power, that energy can become like an entity form, and the process becomes obsessive and destructive. In societies where there has been excessive sexual activity (in the sense of promiscuity or prostitution, rather than in the sense of love), the society is destroyed not through the sexual activity itself, but through the psychic power that manifests through the sexual activity.

People ask me if it matters if they lust after somebody. Yes, it does matter. And what you **do** with that lust matters more. Often the feeling you identify as lust comes into you through psychic influences, rather than through your own consciousness. You may think, "Wow! Where did that thought come from? I wasn't even interested, and all of a sudden I just have to have this girl (or guy)." And often, if that happens, it may not be your thought at all.

A lot of thoughts and psychic influences are around and it's easy to "pick them up." It happens. Keep in mind that you don't have to act on every thought you pick up. If lust comes in, you can get up and move out of that area. Handle it. You can handle it by moving away from it as well as moving toward it. Physical exercise will help disperse psychic energy. Running, jogging, tennis, basketball, construction...anything that uses physical energy in a dynamic, strenuous way will disperse and clear impinging psychic energies. Sitting and dwelling on things in your mind tends to compound them.

Our present prison system is an example of a very poor response to the problem of psychic energies. Before being jailed, many prisoners are already greatly influenced by psychic power. And in our current system, they have little, if any, chance of getting free of that influence. They sit and build up their sexual fantasies, project great energy into them, and then start projecting that energy throughout the prison and the countryside around the prison. This is not necessarily a conscious process; it can be unconscious. The whole area may start experiencing difficulty and be unable to trace the cause. If prisoners were placed in environments where they could be active and work constructively, where they could experience healthy recreational programs and active therapy programs, you would see more rehabilitation.

Many times you treat yourself as a prisoner. You fall under the influence of psychic energies and allow yourself to be held within that power. And if you place yourself in situations and environments where you can be active, work constructively or take part in healthy recreational programs, you will see rehabilitation within your own consciousness.

You do not have to allow the psychic influences to manipulate or control you. You have a choice. You can direct your life into whatever pattern you wish. If you have been under the influence and identity of psychic energies, you can recover the spiritual identity of who you are — who you **really** are. When you have found that center and can maintain that center, you can assist other people from that solid base. You can demonstrate freedom, spiritual love and the Light of Spirit.

As you direct yourself from that positive place within you, you can begin lifting everyone around you into the same positive focus. You can contain and absorb the psychic influences that come into you while continuing to direct yourself in a positive way, lifting into more and more

157

awareness of the Spirit within. It's all your choice. Spirit is always present. You need only turn toward it and open yourself to its guidance and direction, and you will be free.

There is a natural way for us to progress, and then there is the way that is attempting to control and manipulate life. We can look at this in terms of masculine and feminine polarities. The masculine attempts to control and direct his "empire"; he always strives to be in a superior position, the "macho" consciousness. The feminine doesn't have to do any of this because she is flowing in a more natural harmony with everything around, so there is no need for rules and regulations and usurpation of power.

What we need to do is to blend the negative and positive polarities to come into the balance of a neutral consciousness where we can maintain and hold the power of our own self while flowing very naturally with all things around us. We take the best of both the masculine and feminine consciousnesses and blend them. Yes, it is ideal; and yes, it is possible.

Nature progresses in a very natural way which does not exclude the evolution of man. Some people ask, "What about the missing link?" There is no missing link. There are bridges of one race to another race to another race, and after a new race is established, there is no need for the "bridge." We are in a bridging race right now on this planet. At some future point, many types of people now on the planet will be gone. There will be no sign of them; this level will be pulled away. There will be nothing to indicate that it was present, but the new race will be present. Don't misunderstand—we are not dealing in time concepts of two days or two years; we are dealing in the concept of thousands and thousands of years.

Of course, records will be kept of all this, so there will be indicators of man's evolutionary progression—evolutionary in terms of going within to know all the levels with which we are involved while in the physical body: first, the physical; then, the imagination, the emotions, the mind, the unconscious and the Soul. When you have established that awareness within, then you can move to the outer levels and find that the outer spiritual world directly aligns with the inner kingdom. And at that point, you understand what it is all about. The understanding surpasses everything and brings with it peace and tranquility. You may not be aware of that when you focus onto the physical body since the physical body is usually in a state of excitation. It is here to move. Individuals who sit in yogic positions until their legs become useless have violated the laws of the physical level. Many who have been called great spiritual masters have died of cancer and malnutrition because they violated the premise of the physical level, which is to know the physical level.

Branches of science like medicine, or the healing arts, are designed to know this physical body. The psychological sciences were designed to know the psyche or the Soul, but they have become more a study of the behaviors of the body. Sociology is the study of the interaction of these bodies. And the psychiatrists are trying to deal with the interactions of the mind, emotions and body. That leaves those who are on a spiritual path to integrate it all from the premise of spiritual health, letting the spiritual energy flow through all the levels, bringing the total upliftment of man's consciousness.

It is really quite nice to be close with people who are in the physical healing arts, because things like massage and tender loving care can certainly alleviate pain and discomfort. Sometimes to go to a doctor and find out that he cares can make you feel a lot better. Just knowing that somebody cares can help you get rid of illnesses almost immediately. It's very important to have loving care, and loving care is the spiritual action.

Every person is responsible for their total beingness.

159

This does not mean that we don't assist one another by scratching backs or getting a friend a glass of water or giving them a ride downtown. It means we do all of these things—**as long as it is part of their flow of spiritual upliftment.** So perhaps sometime you **don't** get them the water. Instead, you say, "There is the water tap, and there is the glass; help yourself." That can make them feel less dependent and more secure in their own abilities and confidence level. We often do this with youngsters so they can gain experience and increase their confidence.

Too often, when you gain a little bit of spiritual knowledge, you want to grab people and lift them up real fast. But what happens when you grab them is that they trip and fall, and then they become very fearful of your approach to life. Life is very natural, very simple. You make it complex by releasing energies inside of you through forms of symbology, through mentalizing and through wrong attitudes. And then a struggle goes on inside of you, and, not wanting the struggle, you push it back into the unconscious. It struggles there, and then manifests through illness or dis-ease that our present-day sciences cannot cope with, cannot clear. You find yourself in a lot of physical trouble. How can you handle this? You can practice spiritual techniques. There are many of them designed to reach into and clear many levels of consciousness: meditations of various types; spiritual exercises; prayer techniques; forms of contemplation; chanting mantras and tones. These techniques will focus and lift the energies; they tie up the energies to give them form so that you can feel more confident and keep the energies flowing up in a straight line instead of waving in and out.

As you practice spiritual techniques, you become more and more familiar with the flow of energy patterns that manifests within your consciousness. As you become more familiar with the many levels of your consciousness, you feel more comfortable with yourself and with others in relation to yourself. By continually working with the

160

energies inside of you, you learn to recognize what they are, their purpose, their function, their direction. You relax more and more with your own beingness, bringing forward a greater integration of all the levels of yourself. As this happens, you are no longer at the mercy of your physical habit patterns, emotional addictions, mental games, or unconscious urgings. You are able to successfully direct yourself into more positive patterns of behavior and expression.

There are different techniques and points of view about how to get to God, but there is only one way, and that is through your own spiritual awareness and ability to exemplify a spiritual awareness. Often, we hear about Eastern philosophies, Eastern religions, the Eastern way of life. We hear about the Eastern way of life as compared to the Western way of life. People say that Western people are impatient in their search for God, while the Indian or Eastern people are very patient. And people talk about these two different ways. In reality, there is only one way. If you think that there are many ways to lift into the higher realms of consciousness, then maybe you should try some of them to see if they'll work for you.

You'll find when you get right down to the nitty-gritty of life, no one is going to take care of you but yourself. You are placed on the planet with everything that you need already inside of you. Everything is already there. You can't be upset unless you allow it. You can't be controlled unless you allow it. You can't go crazy and lose your mind unless you allow it. You can't be possessed by a disincarnate entity unless you allow it. This puts you in a very unique position. You are a creator. You can create harmony or discord, happiness or despair, joy or depression, productiveness or lack.

161

Overcreating
And Its
Results

I n our Western world, we are faced with the situation of having overcreated in many areas of our lives; we have created too much, too many **things**. Many of those who follow the Eastern philosophy of life have made it a point to under-create. We look at their culture and say, "They're backward. I wouldn't want to live there. They live in filth; there's risk of contagion. There's no modern plumbing system." And we can get pretty self-righteous with this point of view, pretty sure of where we stand in life. After all, we have a beautiful home, a bedroom for each child, two cars in the garage, lovely clothes, fine jewelry, multiple television sets. And we work hard for these things. In many ways, we have a beautiful culture — but one that proves we have overcreated physically. We have all sorts of pollution showing us we have overcreated, that we have too many things. This may be the most significant sign of the times in the Western world. We can be very polite and call it excessive production, but it's really pollution — air pollution, water pollution, plant pollution, etc. These are outer reflections of overcreation, but in many ways, we have polluted our own consciousnesses, too.

Physically, we're quite a well-fed nation. But we have hidden hungers that are not satisfied. You may figure the way to overcome the hidden hungers is to stuff yourself with food until you're satiated and no longer cry out in need. And then you think, "Now I feel better." When you feel better, you think, "I really should do something about getting back to God." You might not think about it in quite those terms; it might be more like, "Now that I feel better, I want to do something. I'm frustrated. I wish I could do something more." Being satisfied on one level, you want to do something now to satisfy another level. Maybe you decide to go wash and polish the car. This helps release the physical energy. While you're doing that, your mind says, "I really would like to read that book I started last night." So your mind goes ahead of you to the book, and you finish the car rather rapidly because you've lost interest in that. You go read the book, but while you're reading, you think, "I'm not getting enough exercise lately. I sit around too much." And by now, it's time to eat again, and this hidden hunger cries out, "Feed me." So you snack on cookies or potato chips or drink a soft drink — anything to satiate the body and eliminate the hidden hunger. But what if this feeling you have isn't hunger? What if you are feeling a lack of fulfillment on another level, a lack of oneness with yourself? When you are not one with yourself, you constantly look for something to make yourself one, to make yourself whole, complete.

You can be alone and still be complete and whole. But it's very difficult to be complete and whole when inside you say, "I am lonely." The loneliness is part of your hidden hunger. The depression, the anxiety and the animosity are all part of the hidden hunger. The hidden hunger is that drive to create, that drive saying, "I want to go have sexual relations. I want to drive a car wildly. I want to go swimming for hours. I want to make a dress. I think I'll take care of the kids for a change. I think I'll go back to school and study. I don't know what I want to do." This is all a manifestation of one situation — your hidden hunger telling you that something is lacking within you.

Whenever you are directing yourself and expressing yourself in any area, you are really trying to show that you are a responsible creator. This is the whole essence of it. You may want to go to school to get good grades, to get an "A". That "A" is part of the creation. It's the fruit of the creation which shows that you're a very worthwhile person. It's something other people can look at and say you're

163

worthwhile. So you go to school and get the "A". People say, "Hey, you're worthwhile" and you agree, "Yes, I'm worthwhile." But a month later something's gnawing at you again. Something keeps pushing.

Sometimes when you don't know what it is that's gnawing at you, you try to think of what it might be. You think and think and think. Then you've overcreated in your thinking, in the mental area. People who overcreate mentally can become giants in various fields of endeavor. But you realize that a lot of the time you seem to go in circles in your thinking. You come to a point where you say, "I've been over this before. I've done this before. I've said this before. I've heard this before. I'm sick and tired of hearing myself talk." So then you say, "I'm going to be quiet for awhile." Maybe that works, or maybe when someone says something to you, you find yourself telling them off and overcreating verbally. So you decide that you're going to get busy and do something physically. You decide to lift weights or run a mile every morning to get in shape. You may overcreate physically. So when you get tired of that, you may move into the area of emotions. It is so easy to overcreate in this area that you can become overwrought when somebody says, "I want to learn to read the phone book," and start crying because of this tremendous emotional overcreation. So you're out of balance again.

At this point, you might say, "I've tried the physical, and I've tried the emotional, and I've tried the mental. There's nothing left to try but the spiritual." So you go to church week after week after week until you get pretty tired of trying to be spiritual. Churches can be beautiful places, and perhaps you can learn to attune to the Spirit there. And yet a lot of religious people seem to have overcreated in mental or emotional areas. And many churches have certainly overcreated physically in building massive church structures. Or maybe the religion has overcreated in the area of ritual so that you think you have to sit a certain way or pay a certain amount of money or say so many penitence repetitions or wear certain clothing or eat certain foods. When you get yourself involved in the type of creation where people tell you their way is the only way, you are not holding fast to your own creativity, to your own oneness. Then you may look at somebody else and say, "Wow! Look how well he's doing." Then your own ambition and greed and lust creep in and you suddenly want to be doing what he's doing instead of what you're to do.

I have watched many people come forward in MSIA. Some of them tap into spiritual awareness very quickly and experience many things that could be called "transcendental." Other people say, "I've been here for a year and haven't experienced that. Why can't I do what he does?" The answer is, he was ready for that experience, and you were not. He walked in and tuned in and made the connection. That doesn't mean that his experience is more or less than yours. The experiences are different. Often the people who seem to be able to come in and move into the spiritual consciousness so easily are the ones who drop away after a few months. The ones who work and work and work at it develop such strength that when they finally receive the glory of their own spiritual consciousness, nothing can shake them from it. And it is so high and so beautiful, it can be hard to believe. Their enlightenment comes from knowledge and work and experience, and no one can take it from them.

Overcreation is an idea you might want to consider. To overcreate in any area causes you to go out of balance with yourself and those around you. You can learn to maintain your balance by creating in the areas of your need, not in the areas of your wants or desires. When you stay in the areas of your need, you find that you do not overcreate, that you establish better communication with yourself leading to greater fulfillment and happiness.

Perceiving
Grace

Your subconscious mind is a very powerful force within your consciousness. Some people try to deny its expression; others give in to it; and still others are simply ignorant of the subconscious mind and its action. When you can learn to work in harmony and cooperation with your subconscious, you can more readily bring your expression into greater balance.

The power of the subconscious is so tremendous that very few things can stand against it, once it gets going. It has a wisdom and a knowledge and a beautiful ability to find its way through all the obstacles placed in front of it, side-stepping the adversities and forging ahead at opportunities.

When your life comes into contact with the lives of others, there is often communication and interaction between the subconscious minds. You may make subconscious attempts to control the other person, and they may make attempts to control you. And deceit can function within these areas of control.

What types of deceit can we express as individuals? We can express the deceit of emotion when someone asks, "Do you love me?" and you say, "Yes," even though you might not love them at that particular time. That's deceit. Maybe you wonder, "Would it be any better to say, 'No, I don't love you right now,' knowing that will upset them, than to say, 'Yes, I do,' knowing that you will love them later on?" There's a good chance that, if you **don't** love them, even when you say you **do** love them, they know you don't. They might respect you more if you'd say, "No, not right now, I don't love you. I think you're the biggest stinker in the whole world. But give me twenty minutes because I'm working on it. I loved you before this, and I'm sure once I get over this irritation, I'll love you again." That's being honest.

There is deceit of the intellect. People may say they know some particular skill in order to get a job. If they don't have the skill, they have entered into deceit. It will catch up with them.

Then there is deceit of the subconscious mind. This is like deceiving yourself. You say, "Yes, I enjoyed spending the evening with you." And the subconscious says, "I didn't. And it will be a long time before I go out with you again!" The subconscious seems to have a "mind of its own." You must learn to cooperate with it and work with it and educate it. If you are deceiving your subconscious mind, you could find yourself starting off on one path of endeavor, then backing off rapidly, because you sense no support from your subconscious.

If the conscious mind is in the habit of starting a project and leaving it before it is completed, then starting another and leaving it half finished, then starting something else, etc., the subconscious may still be attempting to complete each unfinished project to fulfill that which was started. But without the cooperation of the conscious self, the subconscious cannot seem to complete; it cannot accomplish. And it will feel betrayal and deceit. It is important that you do not have too many "irons in the fire." The subconscious cannot handle that. Complete the projects you begin, fulfill the commitments you have made, live up to your promises — then both your subconscious and conscious selves can have success, which leads to a feeling of fulfillment, worthiness and oneness.

When you can be true to yourself, your subconscious mind can also be true. Your conscious self, as master of the household, then reaches down to the subconscious and lifts it up; then both subconscious and conscious can move into the higher expression and function together as a unit for even greater balance and completion.

Man is to have joy everlasting, but man is also held responsible for all his actions. With this in mind, some people say, "I'll just sit and do nothing." That is decision by default because the decisions will be made for you unless you make them yourself. And unless you make the decision to learn from what you're doing, you cannot expect to receive the greater action of Spirit as it comes forward. Great blessings are being showered on the earth daily, every moment, every second. You may say, "Sure, I'm just waiting for the right moment to appear." The right moment has appeared as soon as you've spoken those words, but you deceive yourself. You have to step across the threshold of cooperation and learn to work with yourself, to bring yourself into greater abilities, greater realizations, greater enlightenment.

Ultimately, who do you deceive? Only yourself. You may deceive another person temporarily, but they will find out soon enough. I suppose we can forgive the deceits of the emotions, for there are many reasons why these deceits are brought forward. And we can forgive the deceits of the mind, for there are many reasons why these are brought forward. We can also forgive the deceits between the conscious and subconscious minds. But can we forgive the deceits of one heart to another? When you have committed the totality of your beingness to another person, can you draw back? It really must be "full steam ahead," because many of the things you're working through now that appear to be turmoil and desperation and heartache, may be your joy and happiness tomorrow. The depth to which you feel your despair and your agony is the depth to which you will feel your joy and your harmony. When joy comes to your doorstep, despair is there also. We sometimes wonder at the sadness of parting, but that sadness says we had such a beautiful time together that we will miss the good times.

Everything appears to have two sides to it. If we are like a "teeter-totter" in our lives, it may be that we are striving for balance. We desire many things in life; but as soon as we can maintain a balanced position where what can tear us down and what can build us up join together, we have the greatest defense in times of despair. So often we make our condition worse in our minds than it could ever be in reality. And we've often wondered, "Dear God, how am I going to get through this?" Through "**this**"? What is "**this**"? You're here, which does mean you placed far more importance on your "catastrophes" than they were worth.

God does not allow one thing to come to his children on earth that they cannot handle—not one thing. We've tried sometimes to the full extent of our beingness to see if we can hold up, to see if we can carry a higher consciousness for others. We may be tried in many, many ways. We may be tried by our enemies whom we can defeat with ease because we know who they are and make sure they don't have the ammunition to shoot us down. We have to be more careful of our friends because we place deep, dear trust with them; they are in a position to try us. But it is our loved ones—husbands, wives, children, parents—who really **try** us to the greatest extent of our beingness. They know all our weak points; they know where we are more defenseless and vulnerable. They have the ammunition to do some damage.

If you deceive your loved ones, the disharmony you bring to yourself may be more than you care to handle. It won't be more than you can bear. You can bear it because God has said not one Soul will be lost, not one. It can be a long, long time before you get back to God in conscious awareness. But if you bring your own levels of consciousness—the subconscious mind, the conscious mind, the high self—together in cooperation, if you change your expression and perform into your own perfection, if you do what your Soul stands in need of having done, you can clear past imbalances rapidly.

It is by our works that we are known. If you walk among your fellow men in balance and grace, you become a lifting force to everyone you meet. You lift all men. You may lift them in ways that do not seem brilliant or tremendous; except when the final measure is reckoned, we often find that it was the little thing that really made the difference. The difference may have been made by a pat on the back or someone saying, "Everything's okay." It may have been just a smile at someone who seemed a little low. Or it may have been saying what I call "magic words" to someone. There are six magic words. The first three are, "I love you." And the second three are, "God bless you." They can cause miracles to happen.

Completion is the name
of the game, and that
being so, you might as
well do it now.

Common Sense Is Spiritual Sense

Chapter Eight

The Movement of Spiritual Inner Awareness does not teach **discipline**. The Mystical Traveler Consciousness does not teach **discipline**. Sometimes it brings to people a situation calling for a high degree of selectivity where they must discriminate what their action will produce before they move. When a person is moving into this type of selectivity, discipline comes in as an automatic process. You move from, "I want **my way**," to, "This is the way that will work best." Yet no **discipline** is placed because that is not the way of Spirit.

Spirit offers opportunities. It offers many chances. Some time ago, I was traveling from the Middle East to Europe with some people consciously working in the Light consciousness. Opportunities came up allowing these people to move beyond the point of selectivity and discipline into the area of **selflessness**, not the type where you say, "I know if I do something nice, it will come back to me" — that may actually be selfish. And selfishness will not bring you what you are looking for. **Selflessness** is not even knowing the reward for what you do, or if you did know, you wouldn't do it for that reason.

We were on an airplane, and with us were nine Vietnamese orphans being taken from Vietnam to Paris for adoption. And taking care of them all was one young lady who was very exhausted. The plane was held over fifteen hours in Bombay for repairs, and, of course, hotel accommodations were provided for most of the passengers, but the government wouldn't allow these little children into the country. So they had to sleep on hard floors in the very hot and humid reception area of the airport for about fifteen hours. Then they were put back on the plane, all sick and dehydrated. They had had very little food and were vomiting and had diarrhea. It was heartrending just to look at them. A couple of them looked like they weren't going to make it.

The Light workers all seemed to be drawn toward the back of the plane where these children were; the only thing happening as far as they were concerned was the opportunity to be of service in assisting those less fortunate. As the nurse bathed the children, she'd sort of pass them along. And everyone was very busy dressing them and feeding them and **loving** them and helping them to stabilize the Light in their consciousnesses. One of the little guys, about six or seven months old, wasn't expected to live. I looked at his aura, and it was very depleted. He was very close to death. So the action was placed within the consciousness of the Mystical Traveler. Because the nurse had said, "Yes, I do need help," and the other Light workers had said, "We want to be of service," it was then possible for the Traveler to come in, to transmute and change the probable path. The time appeared that this little one needed greater energy and strength if he were going to live. I placed him with one of the Light bearers, and that youngster who hadn't taken more than a few ounces of food in twenty-four hours, consumed about two bottles of milk in a short time and kept it down. He was coming back strong. He consumed a **lot** of Light and love, too. That little one will probably outlive them all.

As we were getting ready to leave the plane in Paris, I went over and picked him up. (He was my favorite because he was the "underdog.") I told him, "You'll live now; you'll be okay." He just turned toward me and smiled. At

174

that moment, I just sort of dissolved in the love I felt for that child. I felt so much joy and happiness that I was allowed to be of service, that I was allowed to extend the love and Light of Spirit to this child, giving him the chance to more completely fulfill his divine destiny on this planet. And my heart was grateful to all my co-workers who worked with me step-by-step. None faltered.

Joy and happiness are the attributes of God and Spirit. The good feelings are your work made manifest. When you have done your work in the physical world, you have a sense of joy because the work is your love made manifest to other people. Some people say, "I hate my job." If that is your feeling, you certainly do have a challenge, which is to **do** what you dread the most. Since the thing you fear the most will come upon you, it is best to move your consciousness from one of hatred to one of completing the job in the best way you can. In the sense of completeness, you can release the job because it will be finished. If you work in a sense of hatred or despair, you can never complete it because you will always hold some of that feeling to yourself. You'll find that you can't walk away from the work. You'll take it home with you and throw it in your loved one's face. If this is what is happening in your daily pattern, you would be wise to get another job. But it is never wise to quit one job until you have another one lined up. There seems to be a law saying, "If you don't have a job, it's difficult to get one." If you have one job, you can usually get another one rather easily — if you place it out in your consciousness that you want another job.

Often things can come your way very quickly when you place out the need in your consciousness. A girl once mentioned to me that she wanted a lyre but didn't know where to get one. I suggested that she place out her request verbally at an MSIA seminar. She did. I said, "Louder." She asked again. And no sooner did she finish the request than somebody said, "I'll talk to you after the meeting; I know where you can get one." To have it answered so quickly in the physical — that's very fast. Often in my work with people, I hear needs that are placed out in silence, and if it's possible, I meet those needs as quickly as I can. Sometimes a "need" can be met by lifting the person above that need into a higher state of awareness and the need ceases to exist. Maybe it wasn't a need. Maybe it was a want or a desire, or maybe it was a "hidden hunger" that greater awareness fulfilled so that it was no longer perceived as distressful.

You distress yourself. You suppress yourself. You desecrate yourself. No one else can do that to you unless you allow it. You allow it when you work from a point of weakness, a point of insecurity, a point of, "I'm no good." I've heard many people say they're not worth much, not up to much, and so forth and so on; then they bemoan their fate and ask why better things don't happen to them. Who's going to give anything to you when you're not up to much, when you're not worth much?

The opposite pole is to say, "I'm the greatest; there is none greater." That puts out the implication of, "....therefore you can do nothing for me." At either extreme, people find it difficult to relate to you, to interact with you. People want to be free and to be able to relate with you in freedom. Maybe a relationship between two people begins from the position of, "Let's relate to each other verbally; let's see if our philosophies coincide." If they do, maybe you move closer together to see if your emotions balance. If that level balances, you might see if you are harmonious together physically. If that level is harmonious, you might decide to go on to the sexual level; and before you do that, you'd better check to see that you are working from the same spiritual reference point. Without that compatibility, entering into the creative action will just force you into a corner, and you'll reap the whirlwind. You will not manifest Light consciousness. You will not manifest love. You will become the destroyer and attempt to destroy yourself and those around you. That's being very foolish; you don't have it within you to destroy yourself or anyone around you. You just might think you do. You might say, "I can blow my brains out." Remember you said, "**MY** brains," which means that you are more than your brains. You are more than your body. You are much more. The body is going to die sooner or later, but that which is **you** cannot be destroyed. **You** will go on because **you** are eternal. Right now you are in the midst of eternal life. You are living in eternity because eternity is **now.**

When you're living in the **now,** you can accomplish much more than when you try to live in the past or the future. By accomplishing more, you can live through a wider space of time, and things that once seemed formidable to you, now come within your field of accomplishment. You just do what needs to be done. That's living eternity in this moment. And nothing is quite so beautiful.

To live eternity, you must be tuned into the universal force. To tune into that force means that your Spirit within, the God force residing inside you, must tune into the God force that is outside of you — that which is omnipresent and all powerful. As you tune into that forceful, dynamic energy, you will feel the Light move into you. You may feel a tremendous warmth come over you. You may feel very loved for a few moments. You may feel like someone just hugged and cuddled you. You may experience the Light as a feeling of being superman — all powerful and tremendously alive. You might feel silly-happy, like being a little high. If you've been putting a lot of pressure on yourself, running around a lot, involved in a lot of things, you might experience the Light as a calming energy. Its energy may come into you in a very soothing way. You can experience the Light, the force that we call the Spirit, in a lot of different ways.

When you tune into the guiding force that is the Spirit, it does for you what you're too unaware to do for yourself. When you turn yourself over to this higher guidance, you start approaching life a little differently. Because you approach life differently, people around you begin to approach you differently. That has a domino effect, and everything around you seems to shift. For example, let's say that you are holding a bucket of water. If someone hits out at you, he jostles you and the bucket sloshes water all over you. But now you're holding the same bucket of water and as he goes to hit you, you tip the top of the bucket toward him, so that his fist goes in the water. It splashes a little water on him, but none on you. And when he takes his hand out, you can't even tell it's been there. No trace is there. After a few times of that type of "hit," the person will probably stop hitting at you because it's not working; all he ends up doing is getting all wet.

You keep turning the bucket toward "non-resistance," and people hitting at you find out they're not making much of an impression. When they take their fists out of the water, what is left represents their influence on you. When they're not influencing you so much, you become more of yourself. And when you become more of yourself (and less of what others demand), you become less tense. When you become less tense, you release pressure from your auric force field and allow the Spirit to come into you more and more. You build the power of the Light energy around your body.

Attuning To Higher Light

God dwells within you. You cannot find God outside yourself. You must look within to find God. When earth was being created, the wise, old sages asked, 'Where shall we place this tremendous power and energy and Light that is the Spirit of God in man?'' One said, "Let's place it on the highest mountain." The answer was, 'No, man will explore every mountaintop and will find it.'' One said, "Let's place it in the deepest ocean." And the answer was, "No, man will explore there, too, and find it." Where could they place Spirit where it would be protected and only the wise and strong would find it? They decided to put it inside of man — where it would be, simultaneously, easy and difficult to find. Those who found it within would also have the wisdom to use it correctly, to use it with love.

Jesus said that the kingdom of Heaven is within. He also said that the Father resides in Heaven. God does, indeed, reside within you. In a sense, God needs us as much as we need Him because we are the manifestations of God on this level. God lives through all of mankind and through all things on earth. You are a child of God, a son of God, a daughter of God.

As you manifest greater Light and love in this world, you become that child of God in more complete ways. You begin to tune into that Spirit within, that Light, and use it to uplift and bring joy to yourself and others. You tune into the love inside you, that love God has for you, and you use that to bring love to everyone you meet. It's really so simple. It's so simple that you miss it a whole lot of the time.

Jesus manifested in fantastic ways the power of Spirit to which he was attuned. He manifested that he was, indeed, the Son of God. He demonstrated the Light and the love that was within. And look what happened. It is true that when you start to do God's work, those who are of a darker consciousness will try to stop you. They will do everything in their power to block you. When you are expressing the love and the Light within you and someone starts to hit against you, sit down, call in the Light, ask for the power of the Spirit to be placed around you for protection and guidance. It will be there for you. And the thing is that those people who are in darkness, as soon as you turn on the Light, are now in Light. Those who have tremendous power in darkness, if you bring the Light to them, will have that same power in Light.

The only way that darkness will have power over you is if you give yourself over to that force. If you look into the darkness and see your own intolerance, bigotry, prejudice, irritation, depression, hate, disgust, etc., it could have the power to topple you. But if you know that all those things you see are only your false image, not the image of your own true self, then it will not have power over you. You can recognize the false image without giving yourself over to it. Don't give over to confusion. Don't give over to doubt. When those qualities come in to you, ask for the Light. Ask to see the true image of yourself. Ask to be aware of the love and the Light and the energy of Spirit within. It will lift you, and you will find that the power of Light is greater than the power of darkness.

It isn't always easy to tune into the Light. This is a negative planet; we seem accustomed to expressing negatively. If you're driving and someone hits your car, you get out and you're ready to "kill" that other person. You're willing to destroy God's highest creation for a thing that's going to fall apart in a couple of years anyway. You might take a moment to understand the other person is probably as frightened as you, that he didn't want to hit your car and

180

cause pain and confusion for both of you. He didn't want to ruin your car or his car. He's probably as sick inside about it as you are. When you move into that type of understanding, communication can really start flowing between you and that other person who is also God's child. And that exchange of love is more important than the mechanical thing you call **your** car.

In case you don't already know this, it's terrific to ask for the Light to surround and protect your car when you are driving. If you take that energy of Spirit and see it all around your car, you'll find you just won't be having accidents. You may come close, but you'll miss. You may find yourself being extra sharp, becoming aware of all sorts of things you ordinarily don't notice. You might be aware that the fellow in the car ahead is having a fight with his wife....and intuitively you know that following a man who is fighting with his wife is not very safe. You find yourself moving away from him. That's the Light working for you. You might be in a hurry and be pushing your speed up over the limit — and then all of a sudden find yourself driving the speed limit just as a highway patrolman passes you. The Light works in all sorts of ways. The Light may not work for you in big, obvious miracles. But you may find yourself making the right moves at the right times, allowing your life to flow easily into joyful situations.

When you work with the Light, you walk within the most absolute protection that exists. It's so perfect and so absolute that you may not even know you are being guided out of areas potentially disastrous for you. Perhaps you get tied up in traffic or delayed in some other way, and later find out you might have been involved in a tremendous wreck on your route, had you been on time. You've heard stories of people missing a plane for all sorts of strange reasons, and that plane crashes, killing all aboard. The Light in action. When you get delayed or caught up in some unexpected happenstance, you may never be aware when it is the means to protect you from disaster. So don't

181

be too quick to judge your experience. What you see as an irritation may be your greatest protection, the greatest manifestation of Spirit working in your life.

You might think that, using the Light as protection, you should be able to walk down a dark alley in the middle of the night, safe from all harm. But if the Light is really working for you in the highest way, it might not have you walking down a dark alley in the middle of the night. You'll be someplace else, safe from harm. Using the Light does not mean you can be irresponsible in your actions.

The Light works the way it works. It doesn't always work the way you think it should work or the way you would like it to work. It is the most powerful force on the planet and the most powerful force in your life. If you are open to it and develop your awareness of it and learn to flow with it, you find your life unfolding in the most beautiful, dynamic, creative and loving ways imaginable.

Exercising Spiritual Awareness

Many people, as they begin to work with the Light and their own spiritual unfoldment, become involved in a process of meditation or spiritual exercises. These processes are designed to lift you into a more clear state — a place where you are less caught up with the concerns of the world and less involved in the many intricacies of human inter-relationships. Spiritual exercises are designed to give you the opportunity to perceive the reality of your situation more clearly and arrive at some sensible choices for yourself.

There can be some pitfalls, however. People often hear or sense direction during their spiritual exercises. And I am often asked, ''What about the direction I hear inwardly? Sometimes I hear a 'voice' telling me to do something, and I think if it comes through during my spiritual exercises, that means it's clear. Isn't that so?'' And the answer is, ''No, not necessarily.''

I advise people not to be overly anxious to follow the direction they sense during meditation or spiritual exercises. There are many, many different levels and processes activated during spiritual exercises as you move deeper into your own consciousness. And certainly not all reflect clear, positive communication.

A story is told of a man who heard a voice during his meditation directing him to go to Las Vegas — ''Let's go to Las Vegas; we'll make lots of money.'' So he got all of his money and valuables together and left for Las Vegas. He went to the roulette table, took out twenty dollars and waited. The voice inside said, ''Fourteen red,'' so he said,

"Fourteen red." The wheel spun and the ball stopped on fourteen red. He thought, "That's fantastic!" He took his winnings, waited, and the voice said, "Double zero." So he moved all the chips to double zero; the wheel spun and the ball stopped on double zero. He thought, "This is absolutely tremendous!" He had chips spilling over the edge of the table. So he took the deed to his house, the pink slip to his car, all his stock certificates from his briefcase — and put them all together and waited. The voice said, "Thirty-three." So he took everything and put it all on thirty-three. The wheel spun and stopped on twenty-two. He yelled, **"TWENTY-TWO?!?"** And the voice inside said, "Damn!"

That story is indicative of the reliability of many of those voices you hear inwardly. They can be really talkative until something goes wrong. Then you usually don't even hear, "Damn." You hear nothing. Everything is suddenly very silent. And you're left with the responsibility of correcting the error.

Do you really think that the voice within that is your true direction would ever say, "Take all your money and head for Las Vegas"? It may say, "Go check out this idea with your spouse. You'd better counsel with someone to see if this is a wise and practical action for you. Maybe you ought to play the daily double in the newspaper for the next two years without putting out any money and see how it works for you." You say, "Two years? I can't wait that long!" You can't? So go today and lose it all. Then can you wait two years? If you feel like you have to move on something now, it may very well be that your greed is upon you. And then you fail even if you temporarily win. If you're functioning in greed, even your winnings will be a curse upon you; and the first time you lose, you'll plunge into the action again, thinking maybe you can win again. Does greed have any boundaries? Will there ever be enough?

When you hear within you what appears to be an inner direction, an inner guidance, check it out. Be smart on this level. Be practical. Use your common sense. You may be wise to disregard about ninety-nine percent of what you hear. Question in detail about half of the remaining one percent. And the half percent that's left, check out, also, with great detail, to see how it works for you. If you do all that, you'll be in very safe and sound territory. And you don't feel like you've cheated yourself through phony meditation.

Be selective. Attempt to discern the Spirit that you sense communicating with you. Check your levels carefully to see if you can detect where that communication is coming from. Out of past programming by your parents or your school? Out of the basic self attempting to complete some past pattern? Out of a level of fear not wanting to face reality? There are a lot of possibilities.

Sometimes people hear a direction during meditation. Then they take that and amplify it, dramatize it and build on it until it becomes a tremendous "project" they feel they were directed to do. That project may only be an interpretation of the original message, and it may be such a distorted interpretation that it has no relationship to the original. The person who heard the message may be working hard, thinking it's a God-given process of enlightenment — but it may be "false doctrine." People have killed because they thought God directed them to do that. And yet most can look rationally at that action and say, "No way. God would never direct anyone to go out and murder another." But the killer may have thought it was a great idea. I'm sure Hitler thought he had a great idea. Mussolini probably thought he had a great idea, as did Machiavelli. Those are gross examples. But the process can happen in very subtle ways as well as the more obvious ways.

Test the Spirit. Check it out. Look down the road at the consequences and the result of any action you decide to

185

take. Hindsight is often twenty-twenty vision. Look down the road and see if you can activate hindsight prior to the action. Use your common sense. Use the spiritual guidelines that say, "Take care of yourself and take care of others. Don't hurt yourself and don't hurt others." Those are two spiritual guidelines upon which to base your life, two guidelines that will never get you in trouble. Those teachings are of Spirit. Anything telling you to go against those teachings is not of Spirit.

Taking care of yourself first and then taking care of others leads to objectivity in your consciousness. Not hurting yourself and not hurting others also leads to objectivity. Objectivity is watching; it's positive. It's loving. When you are objective, you are loving yourself first. You are taking care of yourself first. The objective point of view is not cold or calculating. It's the free, loving point of view.

The cold, cruel point of view comes from those people who manipulate you against yourself. When they've accomplished their end, they abandon you. As long as you take what they give out, they continue their action. You embrace them, and they use and manipulate you until you submit. When you submit, they start leaving you alone; then you feel better about them and start loving them. They pat you on the back, make you feel good, give you approval and reward you; and you, in your negligent thinking, figure that your goodness and your love saved them. And all along they manipulated you, getting you to submit and give them exactly what they wanted. You think you saved their Souls and changed them. **You've lost**; they'll dump you when they're through with you.

Don't sell yourself short; take care of yourself. Maintain your dignity and self-respect. Maintain your objectivity. If you've played the fool, admit it. Say, "Yeah, I did that." That's being objective and responsible at the same time.

186

It's being objective, too, just to express to people the truth of whatever is present for you. If they tell you something that matches with your experience, it's fine to say, "Yes, I see that. I understand that." If they tell you something that doesn't match, it's fine to say, "That may be true for you, but I can't see it. And because I can't see it, I'm not submitting to it. I am not entering into that process." That's called being true to your own consciousness. It allows you to function within your own loving objectivity.

People often try to get you to go along with their trip. Often they think they hear that "inner direction" more clearly than you do, or they think their idea is better than yours. But theirs may be "false doctrine" from start to finish. That's why you must check out everybody. You must check out me. You must check out my teachings. I've never told anybody to believe me or trust me. That would be nonsense. It would be tempting you to your downfall.

My teaching is and always has been that you must check out all things for yourself. You're free to use whatever works for you. You're free to ignore whatever doesn't work. It doesn't bother me one way or the other, and it shouldn't bother you. The objectivity should be present both ways. And if both people are objective, it's amazing how trust appears. Then, in your giving, it's given back to you. And in my giving, it's given back to me.

My love is based upon my love, not upon what anyone does. It is a love that lifts always. It is a love that can transcend all other levels. But you have to have the wit to see it. You have to have the courage to participate. You have to have the endurance to always turn to the love through all things.

Don't be afraid to look at yourself. If something's wrong, find out **now.** Even if you've spent thirty years expressing a particular way, if it's wrong, it's wrong. Drop it. If you're smart, you'll let it go so fast everybody will wonder what happened.

If you're taking care of yourself, you do those things that are good for you. You do those things that are for your health and your well-being. And you do whatever is necessary to bring yourself into balance and into the love that is your Spirit.

When you are taking care of others, you are objectively involved in their lives and you lovingly support and lift them each moment. You are right there in the moment they need you, and you see clearly what to help them with. You see clearly when to leave them alone, when they must complete and fulfill what they've created. You hold for them as they grow, and when they can accept your love and your Light, you are right there for them. Be objective in your living, and let the love come forward.

Moving Beyond The Timeline

You can block your objectivity, your ability to perceive yourself and others in an objective and clear way, by entering into comparisons: "He meditates longer than I do" — "I do more spiritual exercises than she does" — "Those people are more devoted to God than I am" — "These people aren't so good. Look at what they do." And so on. When you do this, you start looking at everyone as someone to compare yourself with, to see where you fit. **You don't fit anywhere as long as you are in the process of comparison.** There is no place for you. You're sitting on a timeline that extends forward or backward from **today**. Tomorrow, yesterday, tomorrow, yesterday, tomorrow, yesterday — then you never seem to get **here**.

To get right here and now, you ignore the timeline. To do this, first get yourself away from other people, even if you have to put plugs in your ears and a blindfold over your eyes. Do whatever it takes to get rid of all the distractions, the attractive disturbances all around you blocking you from awareness of your **self**. Get your consciousness flowing in one positive, directed stream of energy. Then if you like you can lie down and look into space.

As you tune to your inner Self, you may find that you start getting calm; then you may begin to feel very much **at one** with yourself, and you may start becoming blissed out. Resist the urge to jump up and run to tell someone of your experience. If there's snow all over your face and eyes, you may find it difficult to explain it's because you've been staring into space. If there's water dripping off your eyelashes, you may not sound very credible when you say

189

you've been looking blissfully into rain. Can you really tell people about these levels? You can, of course, but it may be difficult for them to understand.

Have you ever seen someone "space out" while driving in a rainstorm and find it really difficult to maintain the concentration necessary for safe driving? Have you ever gotten "lost" looking into a fire? Have you ever sat by the ocean, watching the waves and listening to the surf until you were just caught up in that moment? These experiences abolish, for a time, the timeline. Time in the conventional sense, time as measured comparatively, ceases to exist for those moments. Some people label this type of phenomena as hypnotic trance. And by inference, they label it "bad." By that same inference, they would rather have you sit and worry about yesterday, tomorrow, yesterday, tomorrow, etc. Is the one who worries better than the one staring into a space where there is no time, only a blissful, uplifted feeling? It's highly doubtful. Worry has never been known to accomplish any great solutions to situations. But moving to a place of "no time" can effectively clear the mind, allowing space for the creative intellect to solve a great deal.

In a state of "no time," you are not unconscious. You may, indeed, be in a very heightened state of consciousness, a very high state of awareness. Don't worry about what you will do when you start to come down. Just go get that blissful feeling. You'll be able to handle the come-down when you come down.....if you come down. There's a good chance that the high you've started with will be your new low; so you get to establish newer, higher highs. Perhaps they'll feel strange or peculiar at first. And you may find people calling you all sorts of names in an attempt to separate you and your experience. If you want to give "weight" to those names, come down and get on their timeline, see what progress you're not making because of last year or last month or the failure that might occur in the next three weeks. Get in with them; it's called the rat race.

As with most things, this process of getting off the timeline can be used positively or negatively. In this world, it's not always appropriate to be "blissed out" in a "no time" space. Ultimately, that space where there is no time and where you can have a clear awareness of your Self is more real than anything else. And while you are living on the physical level, you can also deal with physical reality. So you must learn to move in and out of the timeline, to use both places to your best advantage.

When I was teaching school many years ago, I noticed a lot of youngsters spent much time daydreaming instead of paying attention to the academic materials being presented. Daydreaming gets you off the timeline into a timeless space — but it may not attune you to yourself or lift you to any heightened states of consciousness.

I remember one young man in my class who had stolen thirty-two cars before anyone found out that he **could** steal cars. He was a "dummy" on a lot of levels, but he was sure good at stealing cars. He drove them up a very high cliff and then over the edge, to watch them bounce. I hadn't been aware of this, but one day when I was talking to him, I saw him suddenly "take off" in his consciousness. Having the ability to follow his thought pattern, I decided I'd take a look at this process in which he was involved. The youngster started unraveling a scenario in his mind, and I saw the process involving the car thefts and then his concern about getting caught by the police. In his fantasies, he was outside the timeline. But in the objective reality of the physical, he was set on a timeline that would eventually catch up to him, and he would be apprehended for theft.

Finally I asked, "Why are you so worried?" He admitted, "Because they'll probably catch me on the next car I take." I said, "How are you going to handle that?" He shrugged and said, "I guess I'll just daydream like usual." I said, "Sure, why don't you do that? But in the meantime, I'll bet you I can name more parts of a car than you." That

191

caught his attention, moved him into the timeline of the physical and away from his negative pattern of daydreaming. He said, "You're on!" I said, "I'll supply the pencil and paper and spell the words for you. You name as many parts of the car as you can, and when you're through, I'll get the one you've missed."

He loved the challenge and, at the time, could name more parts of a car than I ever knew existed. He could have beat me a hundred times, but **he** didn't know that; and I had him. We had sheets and sheets of paper filled with names. He finally ran out of parts to name. I imagine he had named every part there was — except **the front windshield**. And of course, I trumped! His oversight was indicative of his state of consciousness.

That challenge happened to be the common ground between me and that youngster. From that start I was able to teach him to spell, to write, to listen, to read and many other things. On that **one** day, I could have said that I was teaching "front windshields." It might not have made a lot of sense to an outside observer, but it was an extremely valid process.

In daydreams, there is no time — no yesterdays, todays or tomorrows. Sometimes meditation is not much more than glorified daydreaming. You think, "Oh, if it could just be like this...." and you mock up the "ideal." For a little while you get out of the river of life; you can look down on yourself as you bob down the river. From the elevated position, you can see that you're going to make it okay, and you can actually plan ahead to by-pass potential disasters. The danger in daydreaming is that you can get so caught in it that it becomes an avoidance — you never come out of it long enough to complete in the physical world, the objective reality.

There is a time and a place for both functioning **on** the timeline and **outside** the timeline. Ideally, there is a balance. Getting off the timeline allows you to lift naturally into an altered state of consciousness from which you can get a different perspective on your life and its relationships. But **staying** off the timeline could cause you to be ineffective in your life pattern and, in extreme cases, could render you incapable of normal, productive life. On the other hand, always maintaining that rigid timeline can become destructive in never allowing space to be "you" — you tend to lose touch with the inner essence of yourself. You tend to get too caught up with outside reference points and outer expectations.

By getting away from your physical body, by getting high enough in consciousness, you find that everything is here and now. When you get high enough, you don't have to stare into space or look into flames; you don't have to daydream or use your imagination. You're out of time from a higher consciousness. You don't look at a back track or a forward track; you see directly — not by way of illusion, hallucination, wishful thinking or urging of your reproductive system. From the higher consciousness, you won't be caught in those lower areas. You'll be high enough to see clearly.

The big challenge then becomes getting back smoothly into the physical consciousness, into the stream of life, moving through all its rapids and currents in full awareness. You learn how to move out of timeline and then back into timeline through practice, practice, practice.

The stream of life is going on, and it's difficult, if not impossible, to get out of it. It must be completed. It is the lesson, and it cannot be avoided. Those who think they are successful in avoidance find later that they reembody into another life to pick up that same level of consciousness and continue on from where they left off. If they're lucky, they **do** continue on and make it.

Completion is the name of the game, and that being

so, you might as well do it now. Handling your life **right now** means you won't have to go into yesterday or tomorrow. You start lifting into a higher consciousness. As you do, you find there is only **one** consciousness. When you are flowing in that consciousness, it matters very little what your physical body does.

The consciousness that is **one** with all is found by going within. The Spirit is within. The Kingdom of Heaven is within. The source of power is within. The Father is in Heaven. If you don't believe me, think of what happens when someone dies. Does the body disappear? No, it stays around; it can be observed. But it doesn't move. That source of its power is gone — that is an inner thing. So we say that the energy that powers the body resides within. It can be called Soul, cosmic energy, electricity, Pranic energy — call it anything you want, but realize that it does exist. This spiritual energy flows from the inside out. So the process of going within — whether you call it spiritual exercises, meditation, contemplation, daydreaming or fishing — can be a difficult process to maintain, because in your attempt to move within, you are actually moving against the stream of energy. It's like an uphill swim.

As you move into meditation, in a passive state of consciousness, you often get caught up by the senses. The mind takes off; the emotions take off; the stomach growls, "I'm hungry!" And you're up out of meditation, out into the world again. The energy has forced you back out. That inner attunement can become very, very hard to hold onto.

Ultimately you can't be kept from that which you are seeking. You will find it at some point. Everyone will find that kingdom within. The heritage and the promise belongs to everyone. Moses parted the Red Sea and Jesus walked on the water, proving that can be done. Their actions put that potential within each human Spirit. In this age, the challenge is to find the spiritual heart, the living love, the Beloved within. We no longer look at the outer miracles as much as the inner miracles of love and truth and brotherhood.

Lay down the ego, and let it be. Let the old things die. And then pick up life anew. You must die to the old timeline and pick up the new one. You drop the old programming and reprogram yourself to the new things you want. The responsibility for this change lies within each person. No one will do it for you. It must be done individually, from the inner heart. Outer forms of ritual or patterned behavior won't necessarily do it. Individually you pull yourself out of the timeline of the masses; you individualize your own spiritual consciousness and then elevate it. There are techniques that can assist. They will not do it for you. A technique only works as long as you work it. When you no longer do it, it can become empty and meaningless. As you reprogram yourself and recondition yourself, you may use many techniques. Some may work for only a short time, but long enough for you to get through to a better technique.

Use everything that works. Use it as long as it works. Then find the next thing that works. The idea is always to keep moving forward into each new experience....because that will lead you into your own spiritual heart and the awareness of God.

You can reside in
the heavenly realms
while your physical
body walks through
this realm clearing
and dissolving
all karmic debts.

There Is More To This Than Meets The Eye

Chapter Nine

The mind of a human being is much like a tape recorder. It records what goes on. And then you spend time isolating and categorizing information for future use. This approach to life can lead to various degrees of grief because much information you receive cannot be catalogued or given any reference point other than "just information." If you try to live sources of "just information," you may be in for a lot of heartache. You can only live your experience. You can only know the validity of your own experience and how to make that work for you.

It is important to realize that the essence of experience is your being involved in time and space in this dimension, and that all things you are bringing to yourself are for your unfoldment. It is important, too, to remember there is no separation between you and Spirit. When I speak of spiritual things, I am not speaking of an invisible action as opposed to a physical action—I am speaking of the totality of beingness. If you separate yourself from Spirit by saying, "I am physical, and Spirit is invisible," you may have placed yourself in judgment of your consciousness. And you might regret that action later.

Many people reach out into the world with the mind, attempting to establish an identity upon which to base their consciousness. This can be folly. You can probably look back over your own life to recognize the truth of that. As soon as you've established your consciousness in some particular area, you soon become a little bored or dissatisfied with that, then you go on to other things to establish your consciousness. But when you reach that new thing, you can again become dissatisfied. Maybe you are satisfied for a little while; but the satisfaction is of short duration, so you get very little rest before running out again into the physical world.

When you cease the mental and physical running hither and thither, when you stop reading every "information" book you can get your hands on, when you stop programming the tape recorder of your mind, then you can know what peace is and let the essence that is divine come forward, moving your consciousness into that which is Spirit. When you have done this, you are in a state of beingness. The mind is quieted. The emotions are quieted. Physical activity is balanced. And you have the potential of entering into a state of bliss.

The blissful state is guarded and protected, and not many people get there. What guards it and protects it is an empty void. When people reach that void, they falter; they stumble and reach out again into the world of illusion and pull "information" to themselves, attempting to establish their identity in the world. It would be nice if that would work, but most of the time it doesn't. The only way I see it could work would be if you had infinite supply of material goods to use or abuse to whatever extent you wanted. Then, if you had a guarantee of living for several thousand years to get through it all, you would complete that experience. Having gone through all things in the physical world, you could then leave it all alone. The **other** way is to go directly into the essence of divine Spirit, reside there, and have all things in spiritual consciousness. That way may be much quicker, if you would care to be a little less greedy and impatient.

When you sit for a few moments and look inward, in

meditation or spiritual exercises, you often stumble over your tape recorder and hit the playback button. And it plays back the miasma of the things you've gone through. You may actually feel like you're throwing up inwardly. It may not be too nice. This process can shake you up. And that shaking can be a form of therapy if it shakes you loose from that which is corrupting your consciousness. When the Holy Spirit, the Light, the Traveler consciousness becomes a vital force in your life, if you have something hidden, you can bet it's going to be thrown up for you to look at. And some people just can't seem to take that. Those who can take it get to make the choice to be free, and this freedom is known by the results, not by just thinking you're free.

If you look at your consciousness as an iceberg planted in the ocean, you know that what you can see is only about ten percent of the totality. Ninety percent is below "see" level. If you felt that you had to chip away or dissolve your iceberg, you might start working at the top where you could see tips obviously protruding. The jagged points could be knocked off in a hurry. You might look at them and realize the weakest areas are those sticking out, not supported by a good, solid foundation. As you knock off those areas that are not secure, you might hear a resounding sound and feel the whole iceberg shake as those parts fall away. And the more you knock off areas that are insecure and out of balance, the more you surface parts of the iceberg previously invisible to you. Then you can work on those areas, also. It may be just as out of balance under "see" level as above. Way too often you have many deeper out-of-balance situations camouflaged with nice, clever words, sharp mentalizing and beautiful illusionary images. All that allows you to not look where you ultimately have to look.

You deal with many levels of consciousness, whether or not you are aware of them. It is to your advantage to know all you can about the levels of your beingness, because then you are able to make more intelligent, conscious choices and decisions and be less at the mercy of circumstances.

Working With The Basic Self

The level we usually communicate on with others is the level of the conscious self—we're conscious of it. But we find out that we're much more than this conscious self, that other levels are within our make-up. Sometimes you "put your foot in your mouth" or find yourself picking up something that you don't need and putting it in your pocket. Why did you say that thing the way you did? Why did you take that thing you didn't need? You know another level is in there that you may have difficulty explaining, yet you can really get involved with it at times. You may lose your temper and "explode," and then wonder, "Why on earth did I do that?" So many situations arise from a level below the conscious level that you're probably somewhat aware, if only by empirical evidence, that another level exists with you. And this level we call the **basic self** or the **lower self**. You can relate it to animal instinct, or to areas of memory or habits or emotions. It's all these things and more.

The high self expresses feelings of great inspiration and high, lofty ideas; it creates the desire to lift mankind in your arms and save everyone. Most of the time, those moments when you see that everything is right and perfect are of the high self. Often this is called inspiration. You might call it a God consciousness, a Universal consciousness or a Christ consciousness; but rather than get hung up in a conflict of terms, we simply call it a high self, a higher consciousness. So every person has within a higher self (inspiration), a conscious self (aspiration), and a basic self (perspiration)—the three selves.

We all might like to express that higher self more often

because it can do the magic. You may know it exists because sometimes **you do** the magic—the way you feel, you can love your spouse, sacrifice for your children or work for hours to help a friend; you can express the inspiration of the high self in a lot of ways. On a conscious level, it may seem like much of the time you're in a quandary of indecision. The conscious self is responsible for making the choices and determining the directions you take. The conscious self and high self can work together and direct themselves rather easily because the high self is spiritual and will choose a spiritual direction, and the conscious self is purifying itself to become spiritual and will aspire to that direction, too. With **Soul Transcendence**, we are speaking of moving the consciousness into the Soul, activating the Soul so it can move more into pure Spirit. When you direct toward Soul Transcendence, you find the conscious self often says, "Yes, I want to do that," but some other level adds, "However, I don't." And those "howevers" are what I'd like to relate to here. These are the blocks that the basic self places in the path of Soul Transcendence.

Let's look at the basic self as being a four or five-year-old you, inside of you, that **seems** to have its own free will which it apparently uses a great deal. Little four and five-year-old children get their feelings hurt very easily. Part of their expression is, "You don't love me; I hate you." Part of their expression is, "Sticks and stones will break your bones..." They go into temper tantrums and rages—"Who do you think you are? You're upsetting me! How dare you interfere with me!?!" Part of their expression looks like revenge. And a great part of their expression is desire. These aren't bad things, in their proper place. But if that were the total force we were working with here, if it had been given complete reign, we'd all be a bunch of animals running around doing anything to anyone and trying to get away free. The conscious self is brought in to balance and to direct the lower self and work as a mediator between the lower self and the high self.

When the basic self is disturbed and can't handle a situation, it wants to have something to do to release its feelings of discomfort and often this is the level of its perspiration. So a lot of times, it wants you to eat a great deal. While you have food in your stomach, the basic self is working to digest the food, so it feels better because it is fulfilling its job. Or it likes you to drink or smoke a great deal because that gives it something to do and quiets it down. Or sometimes the basic self will just tap the hands or jiggle the foot or bite the fingernails—it wants to be doing something.

For the most part, the basic self wants to complete all the things you've left uncompleted. This is a big part of its action. So your job is cut out for you. You complete those physical areas that are the basic self's area of concern. Make the bed, clean the house, write those letters, do the dishes, etc. When you have accomplished what you have to do, it stops pushing you so that you can be quiet and know God. Until the physical areas are handled adequately, it is very difficult to move into the higher levels.

When you take care of things on the physical level and begin to move into the higher levels, the basic self will be functioning well, too; it says, "I like you." And for the first time, you may be saying, "I really love myself; I'm pretty contented. I'm enjoying things. This is a beautiful place." This can be a big break-through. And when you can recognize that this **is** a "beautiful" place and that you don't mind living here, you're really getting ready to handle the inner realms of Light. As long as you say, "The maggots and worms can have this place—I hate it," you will be coming back again and again and again.

That which you fear (hate) will come upon you. That which is your weakness will be thrust upon you so that you can learn to handle it. If you're afraid of the Internal Revenue Service, they're going to audit you. Let them do it. The second time it won't be as bad. The third time you'll know what to do, the fourth time you'll be an old hand at it and then maybe they'll never come back the fifth. You'll be free anyway because by that time, it won't make any difference one way or the other. Tests are not necessarily tribulations. They are areas of revelation. Tests are for you to reveal unto **yourself** where you have to work and what you have to do. You can say, "This is neat," and go toward it and clear it. You can't get away from it so you might just as well go toward it and clear it. Or, if it can't be cleared immediately, maybe you're to learn patience or experience a certain level to learn compassion. There are many possibilities. And all you have to do in any situation is use it to direct yourself in a positive consciousness.

You must work with your basic self in cooperation and love **if** you want its support. If you start berating your basic self, you **can** produce arthritis, rheumatism, cancer, tuberculosis or a lot of other diseases. It's so much nicer to say to your basic self, "You did a rather good job today, and tomorrow we'll do even better." If it has said some unwise things, tell it—"Our impetuosity got us in trouble again; I should have monitored you more closely." And then next time, assert your **conscious** control and keep your mouth shut.

You have to let the basic know that what you are doing is going to make things lighter and easier and more full and complete—"This is good for us. We're doing this to be together." When people talk to themselves, they are, for the most part, talking with their basic selves—"I'll tell them this. I should have said this. Next time, I'll say that." Be careful what you program in because the basic has a great memory and will hold to those patterns that have been programmed in. However, I'm sure that many of you who read the above will be protesting saying, "Oh, no, it was **my** high self I was talking to."

Living
Your Own
Experience

There is another area of human consciousness that might be referred to as the "unconscious." It is an area that may greatly influence your actions and behavior—without your even being aware of it.

Most of us, in this Western society, have been taught that reading is a worthwhile activity and valuable to us. And as a way of gathering information, that may be so. Reading can also greatly affect our subconscious and unconscious levels. The danger in this is that, as you read a lot of books, you may start making the experience of the author your own experience. You start dubbing it in as your own life experience. Before you know it, you're in trouble with your own beingness because you are attributing to yourself experience that someone wrote down in a book. Their experience is not yours. That experience you read about is a facsimile, not the real thing.

When you read a lot of material by people who profess to be on a spiritual path, you may take the experience they have written about and find some place in you that seems to relate to their experience. Then you use **their** experience to amplify your own. And your experience may actually not be the same **at all.** You're dealing with a facsimile which can get you in trouble because, before long, you don't know which is the spiritual energy flow you're working with and which is the make-believe, the duplicate, the facsimile, the counterfeit. That confusion can make it extremely hard for people to progress on their own path, in their own timing. It can block them from Soul Transcendence because they're too involved in the mental machinations of the written word. They just can't get beyond that block. They could be blocked by thinking, "This book is written so clearly. I love the words so much; they were put together so well. It is all so beautiful. Their experience is so magnificent; mine can't compare." They're lost...and that author may not even have **had** the experience of which he writes. It may be an amalgamation from different sources. So that author may have amalgamated a facsimile, produced it as reality and passed it off as his own experience. In addition, those sources from which the author got **his** information may also have been facsimiles. You don't know how far back that process might go. But the result is that you are living a facsimile instead of your real experience. You may say, "But someplace inside of me, I feel that's so true and right." The criteria of spiritual evaluation is not just a feeling! It's a **realization**! Realization produces change through **incitement**. Not "excitement"—that would indicate an outward process. Incitement is inward. It changes the molecules and cells.

If the particular material you have read brings about realization, that realization produces a change inside of you such that you never go back to the original position you were experiencing before you read the material. Then that material has been an **experience** for you and is valid. But if you find yourself back in the same process of seeking and searching as before you read the material, then you have only played a game; you have not enhanced your experience.

The idea of not reading strikes against the very nature of our society and our educational system which says, "Get a good book and read." You read a book to get excitement or some other type of entertainment...but it may not produce realization. It certainly does produce a form of knowledgable repeatability that society has labeled "being educated." "I read **Alice in Wonderland**, and the Mad Hatter said, 'I'm late. I'm late...' " and you are recognized as educated. Being able to repeat things out of a book is not education. True education is realization. The ability to repeat what you have read is memory. It's a mechanical ability. You repeat enough, and you'll get really good at it. It'll amaze everyone how "smart" you are. It may not be smart. It may be rote memory. That's not realization.

This process of creating a facsimile does not apply to reading for information, like reading the newspaper or technical material. But if you are reading true confession magazines or love stories all the time, or if you're getting lost in the last book you read, that is the facsimile. If you've over-identified with Gandalf or Bilbo Baggins, you might be getting **lost**. Pretty soon, everywhere you go you see the mountains of Mirkwood, and you get lost in comparisons and analogies. That's a facsimile. You say, "Well, didn't it really exist sometime, someplace?" Watch out, you could start losing! You're going to try to mock-up a facsimile of a facsimile of a facsimile of a facsimile, and call it reality. It will not produce the **realization** that will produce the incitement that will produce the change...so don't look for it to do that.

This same process of creating a facsimile can happen with movies. And it can happen particularly with television in situation comedies and soap operas and dramatic series, where you follow a character or series of characters for weeks or months through various episodes of their lives. The danger of identifying so heavily with one or more of the characters is that you begin to make their experience your experience, you begin to look for similarities in your life. Perhaps "Leslie's" husband on the series starts staying out late, giving his wife the excuse that he's working late at the office, but he's really got a relationship with another woman. Your husband calls one night to say he has to work late at the office. You immediately move into the facsimile, you move into the "similarity," you move into the illusion, and all of a sudden you are rushing into fears and doubts and worries about your husband, thinking he's out with some other woman.

That soap opera or movie is **not** the experience of your life. The situation of that play is **not** the reality of your husband's expression. There is no similarity. But if you are caught up in that soap opera, you may begin to look for those things in your own life, and anyone can twist things to fit. You're losing.

Be realistic in your approach to reading, films, television and other entertainment media. Realize they are only entertainment, they are only diversion, they are not your experience. There is nothing wrong with entertainment media if you keep them in the proper perspective. But when you begin to use them as substitutes for **your** experience, you can get in trouble, and you may block your growth.

Identifying Unconscious Symbology

With any action, there is almost always the possibility of using it positively or negatively. In entertainment, the negative aspect would be creating the facsimile experience. Yet all the entertainment media can be used for your upliftment and progression, if your approach to them and your attitude toward them is correct. Used properly, entertainment can even be a means to release and clear karmic situations. A film such as, "The Diary of Anne Frank," might have tremendous significance for many people. If you identify with Anne, for instance, and use the experience portrayed in the film as your own experience **for that time**, it is possible to clear karma which might have been related to that time and place in history. **But you let the experience go when you leave the theater!** Perhaps the film gives you a greater sense of humanity, of the oneness of all human experience; perhaps it gives you an empathy and compassion for the Jewish people you never had before. From the film experience, **realization** can result in incitement that brings change. The experience of the film enhances your own experience and sense of self. The result may be more positive. But then you wouldn't go out and look for signs that you are being persecuted; you wouldn't look for signs of violence and hatred in your fellow men. If you did, you used the film as a negative experience that caught you up in its illusion.

Often, at a very early age, you find someone that you look up to for some reason. It may be that they're very macho or very feminine, and you find that attractive. Maybe they cook well or drive well; maybe they're handsome or pretty. For some reason, you like their expression and start emulating facets of their personality.

209

Maybe their laugh is unique—"hu, hu, hu, heh!"—so pretty soon, you're laughing, "hu, hu, hu, heh." You start dropping out your expression and start picking up theirs. Maybe you like another person's walk, so you copy that. And you like the way someone dresses, so you buy clothes with that look. Then later on, when somebody says, "Who are you?" you say, "By golly, I don't know. I guess I'm a little bit of George, a little bit of John, a little bit of Suzie...I sure wish I knew who I was. I wish I knew who was behind all these images." Your expression has become a facade; nobody's home.

You have to be careful, too, when you start into the inner expression of meditation, contemplation or spiritual exercises. You think, "I'd like to meditate, but I just don't feel it's right for me." You're lost! You think, "If I had a quiet place where I could..." Lost again. The mind postures. It accepts a set of criteria not its own. It accepts a facsimile and then attempts to maintain it, hoping that eventually it will produce something good. It won't. That abstract concept that you idealize is going to be your confusion and turmoil and despair until you let it go and return to your experience as your only "valid" reference point.

Can you endure past the facsimiles of your mind? If you see a Light and wonder if that's the Light your guru wrote about in his book, can you let that comparison go, realizing that your experience is uniquely yours and may not "fit in" with another's? If you can, you are changing within yourself—and that's positive growth.

Another way people allow unconscious patterns to influence and shape physical behavior is when they fall into superstitions or beliefs that their lives are guided by symbols and signs. Often people deal with many types of symbology in their lives. They set up different formations of superstitious behavior. For example: if you see a shooting star, you're supposed to make a wish; if you walk under a ladder, you'll have bad luck; if you step on a crack, you'll break your mother's back; if you get to the end of this street before that car gets to that light, then you'll get to go out tonight. These are superstitious formations, symbologies of the unconscious mind, that people hold in their consciousnesses because of unresolved conflicts.

One interesting manifestation of unconscious symbology happens in the game of baseball. Have you ever noticed how certain baseball players, when they go to the plate and are getting ready to swing at the ball, will hit the plate with the bat and look at the bat a certain number of times before they are ready? Or maybe they step into the batter's box, step out, and then step back in. None of that really has much to do with hitting the ball. Hitting the ball is swinging the bat where the ball is coming and making sure that the two connect. How many times they hit the plate or step in and out of the batter's box does not determine whether or not the ball is going to be hit. Those patterns represent a dilemma they are working on out of the unconscious.

Babe Ruth, once a pitcher, used to stick out his tongue every time he was going to throw the ball straight down the middle. It wasn't too long before the rival teams were very aware of this, and their batters would knock that pitch out of the field nearly every time. Finally someone put up a reflector for Babe Ruth and said, "Now throw the ball." As he threw the ball, he watched himself stick out his tongue and said, "I didn't know I did that." Unconscious patterns. From then on he kept his tongue in his mouth. Once you see the unconscious superstition, you can begin to change the pattern.

When you talk about the unconscious and start to put a conscious word level on it, you can start misrepresenting it. The only way you can truly communicate in the unconscious is unconsciously, which sounds like double talk, but it isn't. How can you **know** if you are working out the unresolved layers within the unconscious? There are some distinct reference points you can use. One reference point is an initiate on the unconscious (etheric) level who is traversing that realm. That person has a very good understanding of walking with the unconscious and can give you reference points to it. Another way is to become an initiate into that level yourself and work within the formation of the symbology. Another way would be to use symbology in the superstitious form—through astrology, numerology, palmistry, tea leaf reading, crystal ball gazing, scrying (mirror reading), I Ching, etc. With all those processes, you deal with symbols and forms, letting them reflect to you. You deal with a form of knowing (not intuition) where you have a conviction of the validity of something without having an independent reference point. Some people call it "seat of the pants" thinking; you move toward something simply because "it feels good." It's not armchair philosophy, where you sit and think through various ideas to a logical conclusion.

The etheric level of consciousness (which deals with the unconsciousness of an individual) is an area that has much influence in our thoughts and actions, and because it is unconscious, it's very difficult to recognize where the influence comes from and how it functions. When you work in the area of the occult, many unconscious symbols start coming up into your conscious awareness. They come up in patterns which make it difficult to tell what's really going on. As you tap to these things, your behavior may become erratic; you may appear neurotic. You may experience delusions of grandeur. You may find yourself indulging in patterns of behavior that are very unusual for you.

When these unconscious things surface, there are few reference points for them, and fewer places to put them. They just come up flying. So it is really important not to delve into and dwell in the occult levels unless you can cap these energies as they come up. If you can't, you may have to go to various behavioral scientists, social workers or institutions for medical or psychiatric therapy in an attempt to have these energies capped. The occult level, if you're going to be involved in it at all, should be the scientific, spiritual and intuitive levels—all together. It doesn't seem to be working that way. We seem to have the scientific way, the occult way, and the spiritual way all differentiated from one another.

The unconscious is just another level of consciousness, but it is a level of which you may not be consciously aware. Even to attempt to label it, to call it "unconscious" can become an error in approach because you will know that which is unconscious only through **your** unconscious. The key is to maintain that level so that you can bring awareness there without interference. You do not bring your mind, nor your emotions, nor your body, nor your imagination into it. And these are some of the first steps in neutrality — you just float into the area and allow whatever comes forward to you to be present.

Making the trip into the unconscious can't be done very easily through meditation; it can be done through contemplation. Contemplation is where you take an object and contemplate it, look at it and let it reveal to you what is there. The object does very little except hold still the mind focus, imagination, emotions, vision and so forth. Everything just sort of goes out of focus; when there is no focus, these undercurrent levels start moving up. As they move up, they can release many things. If there are repositories of illness, you may start to go through many forms of memory like, "Oh yes, I remember hurting my shoulder years ago, and it hurts again now, **but not as bad.**" These are the release patterns coming up. When you unfold into these releases and clearings naturally, you experience very little difficulty, because they come forward as you are able to handle them and understand them.

When you go to psychic readers, they may bring forward many things you weren't aware of, but they still may not come out of the unconscious level. They may be coming out of the mental level or the emotional level, and psychic readers can really make you feel good with an emotional interpretation of your unconscious symbology. They can unlock this level for you, and you'll walk away feeling very good toward them; later on, the symbology that your unconsciousness is reflecting to you may start kicking up other symbols and energies. Then you go back to the psychic reader and say, "I've been having difficulty." He may say, "That's interesting. You shouldn't be having difficulty. When I gave you that reading, it felt very good to me." But feelings often betray. And the mental level may say, "But I said everything correctly." And so they rationalize from the levels they know, not realizing they are releasing energies from a more subtle level of which they're not even aware.

Many people have gone to various psychic readers and later come to me for a consultation, and all I do for an hour or more is cap the energies that have been unlocked, because the people are demonstrating that they are not able to handle it. Too often, I will get the energy contained, get the energy capped and get the person feeling good and whole within himself again, only to have him go back to the psychic reader and allow him to uncap the unconscious levels again—and the person may end up in a mental institution. There is such a thing as a "do gooder" who doesn't do good, but likes to think he does good.

Many people may "think" or "feel" that they are very good at reading **other** people's symbology, but often they read them out of their **own** levels of superstitious unconsciousness. Pickpockets see pickpockets. Alcoholics see alcoholics. God sees God. The unconscious sees the unconscious.

It is important not to set up a hierarchy of consciousness for a reference point, but to lay things out on a horizontal continuum. That way you don't have to look at

anything as being good or bad or at the top or bottom —
things are just here and here and here and here. And you
simply approach each thing as a matter-of-fact "here it is."
And if you're saying to yourself, "Oh my God, I have this
thing inside of me. It just keeps coming up — I hear it. And
now I have this symbol in my mind. It's always here. What
is it?" the answer is, "It doesn't matter. There is no way
to know." And if you ask, "What can I do with it?" the
answer is, "Nothing." And if you ask, "How can I get rid
of it?" the answer is, "Get busy and do something
physical." That will resolve the dilemma.

Take your unconscious dilemma, the superstitious
haranguing you do, and run down the street with it.
Physical exercise, believe it or not, can do wonders in
relieving and resolving many dilemmas of the emotional,
mental and unconscious natures. People say, "I know I
need a lot of exercise but running doesn't do it for me; that
isn't the type of exercise I need." I have news for you — if
you run long enough and hard enough, you won't need any
other exercise. That will do it for you. Walking fast can do
it, too, as long as you don't stop, as long as you keep
moving.

One of the biggest keys to spiritual progression in the
physical is simply to keep moving — don't stop. When you
think you've got it made, look around and see where your
next move will take you. When you think you've "arrived,"
look up and get the vision for your next step. Wherever you
find yourself, there will always be another step. Progression is infinite. And at the end of every sentence, though
unwritten, there is always "et cetera."

One way that the unconscious level influences us is in
the formation of attitudes. People often ask, "What is an
attitude? How do I get an attitude? How do I change an
attitude?" Let's look at some of the dynamics in that
process.

When youngsters are born, the unconscious is one of the first levels they express. Then they become aware of touch, and then they become pretty much aware of taste. It can be hard to say which one of these comes first. They are dealing in sensation, excitation and stimulation. For a while, the **consciousness** is pretty much barren. It has a repository that will not be tapped for a long time. The child has to learn its musculature and how to perform in the physical world first, which is its main job for a good many years. When children get older, the attitude starts to be a process of looking and thinking. They look at something and think about it. As they look and think, it becomes familiar. And in the familiarity, they identify with it. And in the identification, they say, "That's mine." If asked why it is theirs, the only "reason" may be, "Because I have seen a lot of it, it's mine." In the mind comes a thought of possessiveness and ownership. The attitude is propped up with a value of "mine" representing "good." And then the value attitude becomes, "This is mine is good is this is mine is good..." It becomes a cycle of possessiveness.

So, often you have to reevaluate the attitudes you hold. Sometimes you reevaluate your attitudes by focusing into another area for a time, by closing your eyes so you simply stop looking. What's the value in that? You won't be seeing a lot of things you don't want to look at. That's one of the blessings of being blind—you don't corrupt the inner vision by the outward stigma of life. You don't have to deal in the same symbology that other people are working through. Blind people deal in their own symbology. They make-believe things so that they can unlock the etheric (or unconscious) levels of their consciousness just as readily as sighted people.

One of the nice things about being deaf is not having to listen to all the backbiting and gossip that goes on in this world; and deaf people may be freer on those levels than many people that hear. People who are deaf aren't upset by hearing things they don't want to hear.

In a similar way, you can consciously shift your focus away from something that is present to you as a "problem" or "dilemma" and break the influence of the unconscious as you change the attitude.

When you enter into the unconscious or etheric level of your consciousness, it might not make much sense to you because nothing is there except symbols. You must be very careful if you are looking through the **astral** consciousness (the imagination) and see things like flying saucers or witches on flying broomsticks or other things like this. Watch that you don't start to think they are really there...that these things are really taking place...because often they are not. It **is** projective imagery you're dealing with. The things you perceive **will** seem so real! They aren't. They're illusionary. Is this to say these things can't exist? If you're talking about "nuts and bolts" type of proof, there isn't too much evidence that they exist; but people who are living in that consciousness of witches and demons are **living** that "reality." Sometimes society looks upon these people as the "fringe element" or the "kooky farm" group. It is your decision as to which areas you frequent. To see the symbology, the images, the illusions, can be really neat, like seeing a painting on the wall; you look at it, then you go on because there isn't too much working reality there. It's a symbolic representation.

Painting has become part of the great symbology of our time. A while ago when the modern, abstract type of art was popular, people were determining whether a painting was good or bad based upon the symbology that would arouse itself out of the subconscious mind or the unconscious level; and they would buy art based upon that. After awhile there got to be so much abstract art that people were being beseiged with it all the time. So the abstract type of painting has backed off in popularity, and we are again finding images that are more solid and real. A lot of the older, classical type of painting is popular again—nature or city or waterfront scenes with people that look like people.

217

Sculpture is still expressing an abstract point of view, and many people who delight in this symbology go to sculptural exhibits to get aroused with this level. It's sometimes like a ferocious tiger in there, and people can get a funny high through the abstract symbology. If it can't maintain itself, however, it can set loose very, very strange vibratory frequencies in a person. And with this, there may be a shift of attitude, and then the consciousness shifts. People may start portraying their dilemma of the unconscious manifestation out here in the physical world as an art form, or perhaps just as a certain type of behavioral expression.

This same process can manifest in dancing. An interesting example of this I observed once when I walked into a record store and there was some music playing; it was what you might call "hard rock." And a little girl about three years old started dancing. She was really moving, and she looked just like a penguin. I said, "That dance must be the 'penguin'," since it was so recognizable. She was really into it, and that symbology stayed with me.

Another time, I was watching a rock television show and observing the symbology that was happening as the young people danced. It was absolutely amazing—it was a cathartic approach, but at the same time, they were unlocking these energies from the unconscious without knowing how to cap or hold them. They may, at some future point, enter into all sorts of weird and anti-social behavior. Naturally this wouldn't be all of them, but because they are dealing in an unknowing way with very powerful energies, they are certainly leaving themselves open to this possibility. Many of them might be institutionalized, not because of anything habitually wrong with them, but because these uncontrolled frequencies are moving inside of them. They tap into that energy, the energy takes over, and there is no place to handle it in this world; so they start expressing bizarre behavior. They may talk nonsense, laugh, giggle, express themselves in ways unintelligible to most people. To them it's **real**; but to others, it's "crazy." They are really out of balance, out of balance with their own form, which is peace and harmony and Light.

The human consciousness has a rhythm and a natural pace at which it evolves. In its own proper timing, it comes into greater and greater realizations about its true nature. It is designed to evolve into self-realization and the awareness of God. Artificial attempts to speed up the process often result in delay and digression. If your path is self-awareness and God awareness, it is best to select the natural methods of meditation, contemplation, spiritual exercises, study with enlightened teachers and association with others also on the path of spiritual awareness. Your progress will be smoother and quicker than with the so-called "shortcuts."

Reaching
Higher

The Soul attempts to gain experience any way it can. It attempts to use *every* medium to observe, identify, experience. And it may get lost in that experiencing. If you have been caught up in a facsimile through reading, films, "hero worship" or another pattern of the unconscious, it may take some time for you to step free of those patterns and feel the freedom of your self coming forward. Hang in there with it. Let the mind energy just disperse. Don't reinforce it. Don't look for your inner experience to fit the way you read it in a book. If an author is being "truthful," he'll tell you his words are inadequate to describe his experience. Yet you will take his words as being the ultimate and limit yourself to the level of his words. That's very restrictive to yourself as the divine child of God that you are. Your experience is so much greater than anything you could ever read in a book. Just because it's been written down doesn't mean that you have to think it's particularly special — for you. Certainly it was special to the **author**. Only **your** experience will be special to you. And ultimately it is **your** experience that will be your teacher.

It takes great courage to see the face of God within you. To see the face of God, you must go in very deeply, past all the things that camouflage reality for you, all the things that have frozen up inside of you, all the blocks that you have placed in the path of your own freedom. And you must confront and clear them all.

The very thing that will free you, the shaking loose of all illusion, is the very thing you run from. Yes, it may be "terrible." And yes, you may be miserable. But THANK

GOD, because now you can see more clearly. Don't run away or paint the process bad or evil. If you do that, you may be painting yourself right out of the picture. Ultimately, you're going to have to come back to whatever area it is that frightens you and look. It doesn't cost one penny to look. The mind may say, "What will other people think?" You know what other people will think because you've been on that side often enough, thinking about others. And your thoughts didn't "hurt" them; they went right on. And so will you go right on, regardless of what people think.

If you want to take the "best trip," go to the essence that is the Spirit in its pure form. When you get to that point, you can "push a lot of buttons" and dissolve a lot of "problems" rapidly. That process of turning inward to Spirit to release blocks will get you as far as the mental realm, maybe even the etheric realm, in your unfoldment. Some may even luck into the Soul Realm, their own inner realm of the Soul. To get from that into the greater Over-soul takes a different process, which we refer to as the Mystical Traveler consciousness. Through that consciousness, you can reach into the Holy Spirit; and through the grace of God that is extended to you, you can then reach into that realm which is your home. When you get "home," you can then work back into this realm, dissolving other things as necessary. You can reside in the heavenly realms while your physical body walks through this realm, clearing and dissolving all karmic debts.

The heavenly realm of the Soul is perfect; anything less than that is not perfect, nor is it the heavenly realm. There are errors on all lower realms. In some dimension, in some state of movement, there are always errors. It may seem perfect for a time, but eventually the errors become evident. There are certainly errors here on the physical realm. All you have to do is look at the way physical bodies fall apart. All you have to do is watch how people misplace emotions, or listen to how information comes tumbling out. Passing on information is so tricky because almost as soon as you start talking about anything, it becomes fraught with illusion and lies and misinterpretations.

Go always to your own experience, to those things that work for you. If you try to get what is working for someone else, you get caught in the trap of glamour which blinds you with magnetic Light so that you do not see the spiritual qualities; then you may really be hung up for quite some time. Have you ever seen people who say, "I must be here to do something magnificent on this planet, to perform a great mission. I don't know what it is yet, but I have to do something great"? They are not going to do anything except run from point to point, circle back on themselves and say, "My God, here I am again, right back where I started." At some point, they'll probably say, "Who needs it?" and let it go—sometimes out of disgust, sometimes out of hurt—but **whatever** gets them to let go is cause for rejoicing. When they do let go, they can become aware of where they live as a spiritual quality, a pure form. Then the world comes toward them, and they perform their destiny from a spiritual state, maybe discovering that they **are** great spiritual leaders—not because they are out soliciting devotees, but because people will follow Spirit where they find it.

When you find Spirit, you will find me also, because that is where I live. When you follow a spiritual leader who resides in Spirit, you follow all spiritual leaders who reside in Spirit. There is NO conflict among spiritual teachers. There may be conflict among their followers. Or there may be conflict among people who think they are spiritual teachers, but in fact **are not.** Those false spiritual teachers become self-evident in the due course of time. They're not difficult to find. Remember, anyone who resided in the pure spiritual quality all the time would be dead to the physical world. Even the most evolved spiritual teachers must come back to this world at various points in consciousness to work on this level.

Imperfection lies in your attitude, which comes from the programmed mind; that's what stirs up the confusion. Sometimes if you just stop thinking for awhile, things can get very nice for you. You can get so many things done because there are few problems when you are not saying "good" or "bad" to every situation. When you just say, "There it is," it's easy. Now, you don't play the fool and close your eyes to the reality of your situation. But knowing something exists, and giving energy into that, happen to be two different approaches. I can very rapidly name off a lot of things that exist that you might not give any energy into at all: houses, television sets, radios, horses, typewriters. You know those things exist, but you probably didn't react in any particular way to them. If I talk about a nice, thick, juicy steak, grilled perfectly and smothered in mushrooms and onions — or for you vegetarians, fresh, hot lentil soup — you might notice that you start to get something of a reaction inwardly. And for some of you, that doesn't do anything, either. When you can be aware of something and not get caught up in it, you are living in a consciousness of detachment, which can be very, very nice.

As you learn how to **do** and then drop all judgment of that doing, you will find the golden path to your own salvation. It is nice to know that, to a great extent, you can do it yourself. And if you don't know how to do it now, then you will evolve to where you do know how. It's nice to know that there are infinite chances. And it's nice to know that you get to create for yourself those things that you want.

Some of us have been to this realm in consciousness many, many times. We are the elders who have made a lot of mistakes through many lifetimes. With those errors has come some greater awarenesses, some wisdom. And yet, the paradox is that the Soul does not necessarily evolve; it just adds to itself the pure essence of what comes to it. So the more purity you can perceive, the more you can add to the glory of the Light you manifest.

223

As you attune to the Light and regularly manifest more Light in your consciousness, you may encounter more specifically the negative force that resides within people. In many people the negative force is predominant. So when the Light consciousness comes to it, it comes into confrontation. If the negative force in others is stronger than your spiritual Light, then you need reinforcements.

If you find yourself needing assistance, I am available to assist when **you ask** for that in the inner consciousness. The spiritual quality that is the Mystical Traveler may come forward, and at that particular point, the negative force becomes self-defeating, because it turns against itself. The Mystical consciousness reflects to the negativity exactly what it is; so it fights itself in the reflected, false image until it's so sick and tired of that, it gives up. Then the spiritual quality may come forward into expression and manifestation.

When you find yourself in conflict with another human being, it is often best to just hold steady in your consciousness, not reacting, until the spiritual quality comes into the situation and presents a mirror for the negativity to see itself. When people get tired of throwing up their negativity, they either leave the situation—which is fine—or they drop the negativity—which is fine.

Either way, they know that the Light force is love and strength. And you will be tested to see if you can withstand the "slings and arrows of outrageous fortune" that will be directed against you, and if you have a spiritual quality (and you do) you find that you can turn the slings and arrows into the Light, which then uses them as "cupid's arrows" and sends them right back to the negative force. And you remain neutral and detached. You don't have to push. You don't have to force. You just let your own Light shine. And those who can see it will know its truth.

Baruch Bashan
(The Blessings Already Are)

the Way Out Book Index

COSMOGENESIS
Cos•mos: n. Universe
Gen••e•sis: n. Origin

The index to the *Way Out Book* is the first tool to emerge from MSIA's Cosmogenesis project. This project, quietly evolving through the years, involves uniting and organizing the information John-Roger has presented in his hundreds of seminars around the world.

This index may be used for many purposes. It lists topics for research and advanced study of the Traveler's teachings. It is a tool for cross-referencing material presented in the *Way Out Book*. It may be used to search out answers to personal, professional, and spiritual questions, enabling us to use the *Way Out Book* as a source of counsel.

Covering many areas of our physical and spiritual lives, the major subjects offered for study are summarized in the book's chapter titles: The Kingdom Lies Within . . . Spirit Is a Process of Now . . . Discover Loving . . . Karma Is Spelled S.T.U.P.I.D . . . Everybody Wins . . . You Are Your Responsibility . . . Taking Care of Yourself . . . Common Sense Is Spiritual Sense . . . There's More to This Than Meets the Eye.

Yes, there *is* more to this than meets the eye. Through the subtle teachings of the Traveler, we are given access to all knowledge. That knowledge resides within our hearts. The *Way Out Book Index* is a guide for tapping into that inner knowledge.

This index to the *Way Out Book* alphabetically lists the book's main subjects and their page numbers. It emphasizes the techniques and keys to which John-Roger refers on pages 1 and 6. Both "Technique" and "Key to" are frequently used subheadings.

Alphabetical arrangement is word by word (e.g., "Spiritual vision" comes before "Spirituality"). *See* and *See also* cross-references are provided to lead to other selected index headings and to indicate related index headings. Parenthetical phrases are added to clarify the use of a subject heading, for example, "Spiritual worlds (ninety percent)." The term *passim* is used after a sequence of page numbers (e.g., 42-61 passim) to denote that the subject is referred to, not continuously, but in scattered passages throughout those pages of the text.

231

G

258

S

S

S

S

S

S

S

S

271

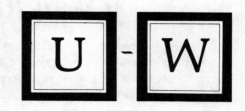

JOHN-ROGER

John-Roger is the founder and current spiritual director of the Movement of Spiritual Inner Awareness. He brings to his work an educational background in psychology and over 20 years of counseling, teaching, writing, and speaking. Most important, he shares from his experience and can assist others in awakening to their own connection to Spirit.

Like many of us, John-Roger began his journey long before he knew about it himself. It wasn't until a serious accident in 1963, when he had a near-death experience, that he had a startling transformation of consciousness. At that time, John-Roger became what many would call self-realized, yet it was something more. His awakened self led him into a life of service and, more significantly, a path of loving. This consciousness of unconditional loving that he manifests became known as the Mystical Traveler Consciousness.

In explaining what this consciousness is, John-Roger has said that "the nature of the Mystical Traveler is love, joy, and upliftment. It brings health, wealth, and happiness on the physical level, calm to the emotional level, peace to the mental level, ability to the unconscious level, and fulfillment to the spiritual level by awakening the divine heritage in each person."

In addition to his role as founder and spiritual director of MSIA, John-Roger is also founder of Prana Theological Seminary and College of Philosophy, a school for spiritual studies; the Heartfelt Foundation, dedicated to community service; Baraka Center, a holistic healing and research clinic; Insight Transformational Seminars, offering a range of personal growth seminars; Koh-E-Nor University, a fully approved, degree-granting university; Integrity Foundation, dedicated to promoting personal integrity; and the John-Roger Foundation, sponsor of the International Integrity Award. The JRF is also the flagship organization that provides support to the above organizations as well as to other groups and individuals involved with education, health, science, research, community service, and the study of individual and world peace.

BOOKS BY JOHN-ROGER

Title	Order#	Donation
A Consciousness of Wealth: Creating a Money Magnet (Softbound)	951-3	$5
Inner Worlds of Meditation (Softbound)	977-7	$5
Passage Into Spirit (Softbound)	25-4S	$8
(Hardbound)	25-4H	$12
The Power Within You (Softbound)	24-6	$8

TAPES BY JOHN-ROGER

Title	Order#	Donation
Integrity: One From the Heart	7154 (audio)	$ 8.00
	V-7154 (video)	$50.00
Mending a Broken Heart?	2145 (audio)	$ 8.00
The Wayshower (2 cassette packet)	3901 (audio)	$15.00

The above are only a few of the many publications and hundreds of cassettes recorded during John-Roger's sharing of the teachings in seminars throughout the world. (For locations of tape seminars in your area, please write to us.) Audio and video cassettes of these seminars are available. To place orders for cassettes, publications or a catalogue of John-Roger's material, please write to:

The Movement of Spiritual Inner Awareness®
P.O. Box 3935, Los Angeles, CA 90051
(213) 737-4055

World economics may change suggested donations.